MIND
YOUR
BUSINESS

To my parents, Theo and Marie Vorster,
my wife, Anneke, and my daughter, Mia.

Theo Vorster

MIND YOUR YOUR BUSINESS

Advice from South Africa's
top business leaders

JONATHAN BALL PUBLISHERS
Johannesburg & Cape Town

Author's note:
Information on companies reflects the state of affairs as at the date
on which the interview was broadcast, and covers the experience that was
shared during the interview.

First published in 2013 by
JONATHAN BALL PUBLISHERS
a division of Media24 Limited
P O Box 33977
Jeppestown
2043

ISBN 978-1-86842-600-3
Also available as an ebook
ISBN 978-1-86842-297-5

Translation from Afrikaans by Linde Dietrich
Cover design and typesetting by MR Design, Cape Town
Set in Garamond Book 11pt
Printed and bound by Paarl Media

Twitter: http://www.twitter.com/JonathanBallPub
Facebook: http://www.facebook.com/pages/Jonathan-Ball-Publishers/298034457992
Blog: http://jonathanball.bookslive.co.za/

Contents

FOREWORD

The need for leadership is one of the most pressing challenges facing our society today. What defines good leadership? Is there a blueprint? Are international leadership formulas applicable to us here in Africa and, more specifically, in South Africa?

Internationally, there is a plethora of books on leadership and the road to success, from Don Miguel Ruiz's *The Four Agreements* to John Maxwell's *Developing the Leader Within You* and Stephen Covey's *The 7 Habits of Highly Effective People*. Locally, however, the topic has not yet been thrashed out properly, especially when it comes to spotlighting our own successful business leaders and their unique achievements.

We are privileged to have some of the most successful business leaders in our own country. They operate in the here and now, and demonstrate to us how they have managed to achieve success in a country with so many distinctive challenges. These resourceful individuals are worthy of emulation, and their success stories are directly applicable to everyone who wants to build a future in South Africa.

Theo Vorster and the *Sakegesprek* programme have brought this important content to kykNET. The conversations with our homegrown business leaders have opened up new worlds that we can identify with and relate to. I believe that many readers and viewers will be able to apply these recipes in their own endeavours, and that this will lead them to even greater heights and more job opportunities. Business leadership is of greater significance than political leadership. The one puts bread on the table while the other gets stuck in bureaucracy and endless arguments. I am proud of the outstanding entrepreneurs and business leaders that our country has produced. It is a privilege to document their stories, so that as many new businesspeople as possible can learn from their conclusions and experiences.

Karen Meiring
Director of Afrikaans channels at DStv

INTRODUCTION

The best teacher has always been personal stories, in which people share their real-life experiences and relate what they did right in order to achieve success and overcome setbacks. The idea behind the television programme *Sakegesprek met Theo Vorster* was to interview successful South African businesspeople about their personal career stories.

It was important that the business leaders should cover a wide spectrum – from entrepreneurs to professional business managers, from multi-billion-rand companies to smaller niche firms, from businesses in a growth phase to mature conglomerates that dominate their markets. The guests had to include established business leaders reflecting on long careers as well as up-and-coming younger people who are making a name for themselves – from the veterans you read about in academic studies to the successful whizz kid who may have been at school with you.

The programme concept was premised on the inspiring value of role models. In our contemporary world, we are quick to turn celebrities into role models – usually completely outside their field of expertise. But it is nonsensical and unfair to expect individuals who excel at hitting sixes or kicking a rugby ball to be role models in other spheres, or to serve as examples to people when it comes to their businesses or careers.

Most of us will spend the major part of our lives in a working or business environment. If you want to be successful in your career or your own business, rather listen to someone who has excelled in that particular environment than to the guy who has made his mark on the sports field.

In January 2010 I presented the concept to Karen Meiring and Marida Swanepoel at kykNET's offices in Randburg. The channel agreed at once to broadcast the programme, and Marida was appointed as supervisory producer.

Dirk Mostert proved to be an excellent choice as producer; besides his experience, he was sufficiently senior to be able to communicate well with the business leaders (in other words, to dictate to our guests where and how they had to sit, speak and look). Dirk and his colleague Rudi Ahlstrom are always prepared to make changes at short notice to their schedules, the programmes and the content. The project would not have worked in the hands of someone who would have wanted to change the concept or make me do something with which I might disagree.

Once I had received the go-ahead, however, the burning question was whether I could persuade the right people to be guests on a brand-new and untested television programme, and how they would react when I contacted them. On a Friday afternoon I invited my first prospective guests. I sent emails to five prominent business leaders, kept my fingers crossed, and immediately started agonising – what would I do if no one had responded by Monday afternoon? At what stage would I devise a plan B (or C or D), and what exactly would these plans look like? From a practical perspective, we had to shoot our first interview in the next two to three weeks to keep to the agreed time schedules.

I was astounded when I checked my email later that afternoon; all five people had replied, and all the responses were positive! By the way, over the three series almost everyone who was invited agreed to participate in the programme.

My first guest was Laurie Dippenaar, co-founder and current non-executive chairman of the FirstRand Group. As Laurie first wanted to talk to me about the programme and get an idea of what I wanted to achieve with it, he invited me for lunch on the day before we were to shoot the formal interview.

Laurie had also asked me beforehand to send him a broad outline of the topics I intended to cover, which I did. When we sat down to our lunch, I was anxious to hear his verdict on my emails and on the notes that he had brought along.

We spent probably around five minutes discussing the programme before chatting for the next two hours about rugby, South African politics, the global economy and other issues. He spoke to me as if I were a long-standing confidant. This conversation was a precursor of my first interview, and I understand now why Laurie is considered someone of irreproachable stature in the business world.

A useful tip that emerged from this lunch was that I should inform the business leaders beforehand about the questions I intended to ask in order to give them time to reflect properly on the core elements of their answers. As Laurie put it, he didn't relish the idea of driving home after the interview and realising when he was halfway there what the most appropriate answer would have been. I try to apply this principle always, and have found that guests tend to be relaxed and well prepared if they believe that you have done your homework properly.

The first third of the *Sakegesprek* programme consists of a discussion of the week's most important business news. Journalists from Sake24 – initially Ryk van Niekerk in the first series and subsequently Riana de Lange in the second and third series – have added in-depth knowledge and quality to this segment. I remain impressed by the expertise and thorough preparation of these senior journalists.

The first series was exceptionally successful. *Sakegesprek* was consistently among kykNET's top 20 weekly programmes, which was also the case with the two follow-up series. Of even greater value to me was the fact that it was among the few programmes on this list that was broadcast after 21:00, and also one of the very few that was not primarily regarded as light entertainment.

In the first series we conducted a very good interview with Louis von Zeuner, who was still Absa's deputy chief executive at the time. Louis was the first, as well as the only, person I approached about sponsorship of the two follow-up series. He informed us straightaway that Absa would like to be involved. I really have to thank Louis, and later also Willie Lategan and Izak Smit, for their support of the programme. It made me realise once again that businesses and business decisions ultimately depend on the individuals who have to steer the ship.

Each of the 38 chapters of this book consists of a summarised version of a particular interview, through which I attempt to highlight each business leader's unique recipe for success and to draw lessons from his or her experience. This is by no means an exhaustive or representative list of star performers. I could easily do ten more series. South Africa has no shortage of business achievers with inspiring personal success stories – I hope to talk to more of them in the next series.

In the concluding chapter I briefly highlight some of the core points that have struck me over the course of the three series. The stories contain certain elements that are unique to each individual, but there are also common elements that cropped up repeatedly. From these common elements I have drawn 'seven golden rules for success' that, to my mind, encapsulate the most significant lessons from these 38 business leaders' stories.

CHAPTER 1

Laurie Dippenaar

CO-FOUNDER AND NON-EXECUTIVE CHAIRMAN OF THE FIRSTRAND GROUP | *Interview broadcast on 5 July 2011*

After qualifying as a chartered accountant and working at the Industrial Development Corporation (IDC) for three years, Laurie co-founded Rand Consolidated Investments in 1977 with Paul Harris and GT Ferreira. Over time, this trio has built one of South Africa's most successful financial services groups, through strategic takeovers (eg Rand Merchant Bank, Momentum, Southern Life and First National Bank) and by starting and growing new businesses such as OUTsurance and Discovery. Today the FirstRand Group has a market value exceeding R160 billion, 45 000 employees, and more than R1 trillion in assets under management.

What stands out during an interview with Laurie is the ease with which he deals with the questions and topics, and how relaxed he appears in front of the cameras. Another striking feature is his reasoned approach to any topic: first contextualising his answer, then highlighting the key points, and ending with a logical conclusion – as if it couldn't have happened any other way.

When one looks at the success he has achieved, it is easy to forget how and where it all started. I wanted to get an idea of what it was like in the beginning, before there was money in the bank. Laurie makes no bones about the modest start of FirstRand's predecessor, Rand Consolidated Investments (RCI), in 1977. Paul Harris, GT Ferreira and Laurie kicked off their business with R10 000 – about R70 000 in 'today's money', he says. 'We had a few good product ideas that worked, and for nine months none of us drew a salary because there simply wasn't enough money. People often ask me whether we had any idea at the time of where we would be today. Absolutely not; we were just trying to survive, limiting costs wherever we could.'

According to Laurie, they were 'too small and too poor even to afford a photocopier'. Their offices happened to be situated above a copy shop; whenever something had to be copied, 'you had to take the lift to the ground floor, go into the shop, get your copy made, and traipse up again. After a few months, GT told me that this wouldn't do – we had to buy our own photocopier.' When Laurie explained that he was in charge of their finances and that there was no money for such a luxury, GT offered to buy a photocopier out of his own pocket – they just had to pay him the same amount per copy that the shop charged. Laurie relates that he did the sums and realised GT would pay off his machine within three months. 'So I said, no, let's rather buy our own machine.'

When one looks back on the development of the group, several milestone achievements stand out. With the benefit of hindsight, these steps appear logical, yet each one was a decision taken within the context of the particular time. The first milestone was their acquisition of a banking licence in 1984. When I ask why this was so significant, Laurie explains: 'At that stage, after our start in 1977, we had become fairly big, but we didn't really fall under any particular law.' They felt that this affected the credibility of the organisation, and that they 'had to subject ourselves to some or other form of specific legislation – stock exchange legislation, life insurance, banking or whatever. It was then that we decided the best legislation and vehicle we could use was that of a bank.' And, as he puts it, 'then we had a piece of luck'.

At about the same time that RCI started in 1977, Johann Rupert had bought a 'bankrupt bank', namely, Rand Merchant Bank, from Rand Bank. 'In 1983 his father summoned him and asked him to return to Remgro. He then looked for people who could take over the bank from him, people he trusted and who would in his view handle the staff correctly.' As both Paul and GT had been at university with Johann, his choice fell on their group. 'That was a stroke of luck,' says Laurie, 'because we had tried before to acquire a banking licence and failed, and now this opportunity dropped into our lap.'

The second big milestone I wanted to explore was the takeover of Momentum in 1992, and what this step contributed to the group. Again I received a very logical answer: 'As you know, income from merchant banking can be very erratic and we were looking for something that would give us a more steady income source, so-called annuity income.' Laurie says they identified the insurance industry as the right type of investment to give them such income, and once more 'a piece of luck' came their way. When the then shareholders of Momentum decided to sell the company, 'they came to see us to help them find a buyer. We told them, wait, we are putting up our hand, we'll buy the company, and of course it was a wonderful investment.'

In the late 1990s they acquired Southern Life and First National Bank from Anglo American. This third milestone changed the nature of the group yet again, and again it sounds like a logical next step.

According to Laurie, in 1996, 'after the advent of the new South Africa', the group had already identified the entry of foreign banks into the country as a threat to Rand Merchant Bank. Because they knew that competition from foreign banks was inevitable and that these banks would mostly go after their big corporate clients, they decided they needed a retail bank strategy. As a first step, they bought 20% of the old Natal Building Society (NBS), 'but when we wanted to acquire 50%, they refused. They didn't like these Johannesburg guys; they were a Durban company. So they fled into the hands of Christo Wiese's Boland Bank. Of course this didn't work out very well, as the cultural differences were too great. Interestingly, years later we acquired the Natal Building Society's mortgages book. So the tables were turned.'

After the failed attempt to acquire control of the Natal Building Society, Laurie and his colleagues decided in 1998 to buy Southern Life, 'which was struggling a bit', on the insurance side. Anglo was prepared to sell Southern Life to them, provided that they bought First National Bank as well. 'Luckily, we didn't have to think for too long about this,' says Laurie, 'because we had already identified the retail gap and the strategy. But he admits that the size of the transaction 'frightened us a bit'. At the time it was a big transaction even in global terms, 'and we would suddenly go from 6000 to 30000 people. But it was, in any case, all part of this overall strategy to diversify our income.'

In retrospect, these three milestones all seem obvious. What I find noteworthy is that each transaction was consistent with a strategy. The characteristic feature is that they first decided on a strategy and then kept a lookout for transactions that would fit into it – not the other way round. Laurie exaggerates when he refers to the instances of 'luck'; choosing a strategy and then concluding a transaction that dovetails with it has more to do with the strategy than with luck.

The golden thread that runs throughout the group, and through Laurie's business philosophy, is innovation and the promotion of innovative ideas. When I asked Laurie why FirstRand have managed to achieve things that many others only talk about, his answer made it clear that innovation does not just occur spontaneously within a business. In Laurie's view, it needs to be 'part of the DNA of a company's inherent culture. For this to happen, the right signals and messages have to come from the top.' To illustrate his point, he refers to some of their 'interventions' at Momentum after the takeover in order to change the existing hierarchical company culture, 'which smacked of the civil service', to something more relaxed within which innovation could flourish. They built a graffiti wall on which staff members could put any message they wanted to voice, adapted the dress code ('ties and things like that' were done away with), and introduced a first-come-first-served policy to replace formal, hierarchy-based parking spaces.

First National Bank, explains Laurie, has 'formal interventions aimed at encouraging and rewarding innovation'. There is, for example, an annual bank-wide competition in which employees submit ideas for innovations; after a comprehensive judging process, the person or team that has come up with the best idea can win anything from R1 million to R3 million. 'To summarise: it's a combination of the climate that is created from the top and formal interventions. Both are very important.' He believes that in a business like theirs, where innovation is encouraged, people have 'the right to question and to challenge top management's ideas, policies and strategies, and to conduct a robust debate within the company, but it takes a mature leader that allows himself or herself to be challenged by a more junior person about a strategy.' The point in this regard, he adds, is that 'the debate should be conducted in terms of business-case reasoning. In other words, with no prejudice or preconceptions involved. Only the business principles should apply in that debate.'

A conversation with Laurie Dippenaar leaves you with the realisation that you have talked to a business giant. It is only later, when watching the recording, that you discover he was actually the person in control of the interview from the first to the last word; he knows exactly what message he wants to convey and he puts you, as interviewer, at ease throughout this process. As Laurie says, it's a mature leader that allows people to question him or her – he will obviously allow this and enjoy the debate as well, that's for sure – but don't be fooled into thinking that just showing up is enough; you have to know your stuff!

PRINCIPLES FOR INVESTMENT DECISIONS

- **Compound growth** – investments are about time and the principle of compound interest. 'Those who understand compound interest, earn it; those who don't understand compound interest, pay it.'
- **Investments are about the long term** – 'I'm amazed by the short-term view people take of investments; generally they don't talk of investments, but of a tip – a share that doubles. That's extremely rare.'
- **Stick to brands you can trust** – 'When people are looking for a new car, they keep to well-known brands; when it comes to investment, however, they tend to trust just any brand.'
- **Responsibility** – 'I don't believe in this notion of collective responsibility. It's very popular in politics ... rather give me a situation where two people who feel responsible sign a cheque, than one where ten people sign the cheque and after the second or third signature the guy only signs because the person before him has done so.'
- **Doers vs talkers** – 'Discovery started in 1992 with capital of R10 million and today its value on the stock exchange is R23 billion, but the secret is, of course, to appoint doers, not talkers. It's not my style to peer over someone's shoulder and to ask constantly, "What are you doing? Why aren't you finished?" So, my view is, simply: give people the chance to realise their ideas and then leave them to get on with it, but choose the right people. You should be a doer, not a talker.'

CHAPTER 2

Russell Loubser

FORMER CHIEF EXECUTIVE OF THE JSE
Interview broadcast on 12 July 2011

After his studies at the University of Pretoria and a successful career as executive director of financial markets at Rand Merchant Bank, Russell joined the Johannesburg Stock Exchange (JSE) in 1997 as chief executive. Over the next 15 years, he transformed and modernised the JSE to such an extent that the World Economic Forum ranked it as the world's best-regulated and best-run securities exchange in 2010. At the end of 2011, Russell stepped down as chief executive of JSE Limited, the company that runs the JSE Securities Exchange South Africa, and he currently serves on various boards. He is still one of South Africa's most respected business leaders and does not hesitate to express his views on economic and business issues.

I was involved in the financial markets when Russell was appointed chief executive of the JSE in 1997. People who were not part of that environment don't really have an idea of the fierce and hostile criticism he had to endure. The old Johannesburg Stock Exchange was a closed club with vested interests. Suddenly an outsider arrived with plans for a radical overhaul of this exclusive club.

How did he, as a change agent, experience the resistance? Russell admits that, while some of the initial criticism was often valid, it was in many instances unjustified. 'They had simply become used to the fact that the JSE was bad and didn't operate effectively,' he says. Those first three or four years were hard, 'probably the most difficult time in my entire life'. Fortunately he had a very good background in financial markets, and no one could really give him a satisfactory explanation of what was wrong with that which he and his team aimed to do. 'In fact,' he remarks, 'I knew that what I wanted to do was the right thing. Maybe it was stupidity, or maybe just stubbornness, but I knew what I wanted to accomplish. I knew where I wanted to end up.'

To understand Russell's achievement and the total transformation he brought about, one should compare the JSE of 1997 and the JSE at the end of 2011. In 1997, the JSE had no capital reserves; in 2011, it had more than R1 billion in reserve and could guarantee all transactions. In 1997, less than half of all transactions were settled effectively; in 2011, the effective settlement rate was 99.99%. The cherry on the top came in 2010 when the World Economic Forum rated the JSE as the best-regulated and best-run securities exchange in the world.

In the 1990s, the JSE was opened to corporate membership so that financial institutions could become members and acquire stakes in broking firms; an electronic settlement system was introduced to replace the previous manual settlement of scrip; electronic trading replaced the traditional trading floor; and the instruments were expanded to include various derivative instruments and products. Under Russell's leadership, this club without reserves and with a poor settlement history was converted into a fully electronic exchange with capital reserves, acquiring the reputation of being one of the best-regulated securities exchanges in the world to boot. JSE Limited, the company that runs the JSE, is itself listed on the JSE and is regarded as a blue-chip share.

I wanted to find out from Russell how one gets it right, to steer an exchange at the southern tip of Africa towards world-class excellence. He responded modestly: 'I had a very good team around me, and that team that you assemble is extremely important. And you need to know that you can make mistakes, and I did make mistakes.' An advantage he had, in his view, was the experience he had already acquired when it came to financial markets. Russell refers to 'those 10 000 hours' Malcolm Gladwell talks about in his book *Outliers*, 'which you have to put in if you want to become a good surgeon, a good computer specialist, or whatever'. He reckons that he owes his success to the fact that he had the right people on his team, and that his agenda couldn't be questioned – 'all you want to do is to make things world-class, not Africa-class, because that's not good enough'.

What is striking about this story is the goal Russell set for the JSE. He was not only intent on knocking the JSE into shape; his vision went beyond that. 'If you are situated in this part of Africa,' he says, 'you almost have to be better than other exchanges. That's the fact of the matter, since the expectation is that you are going to be bad.' If you don't settle each and every transaction perfectly, he explains, 'the world regards you as risky' and investors are not going to trade through you. 'There are many other places where they can get hold of shares. They just won't come to South Africa.' According to Russell, they had told themselves from the outset 'that we want to transform this JSE into a world-class exchange in order to completely change and improve financial markets in a country'. In the United States, Europe and most countries in the East, the markets 'are today already fairly good or very good, and they can't be changed any more'. In South Africa, on the other hand, change and improvement were possible. Russell says he considers himself fortunate in having been given the opportunity to change fundamentally a market that was by no means functioning well.

I wanted to know why he had said, in one of his last annual reports, that one should have fun at work, and what he meant by this. His answer centred on the role of his wife, who made it possible for him to enjoy his work; she took the responsibility for the children upon herself and allowed him to fulfil himself at work. He believes the reason why he 'has remained so enthusiastic about the financial markets, about the JSE, about life', is that she made it easy for him to be able to work hard and to have fun at work as well as with her and the family.

The compliment came after the interview when Russell's wife, Alma, contacted me to find out when the interview would be broadcast. In the 15 years Russell had been at the helm of the JSE, he had done a multitude of interviews – this was the only time he had asked Alma to watch one.

What stayed in my memory is that Russell had decided the JSE should be the best exchange in the world, and that nothing less would do. This is what defines Russell: he will never be satisfied with second best.

ADVICE TO YOUNG PEOPLE

- 'Get those academic qualifications, because they are a good starting point and something you will always have – which no one can take away from you.'
- Be prepared to start at the bottom, to put in the hard work (the '10 000 hours') and to acquire the necessary experience.
- Only expect to succeed if you have earned it, 'not because someone says you deserve it because you are white or black or female'.

THE ROLE OF MISTAKES IN BUSINESS

- Realise that you will make mistakes. 'You only learn by making mistakes. If you haven't made any yet, you think you're the best, and you need to make those mistakes, like golfers. You have to be able to come back afterwards and learn from the experience, because it's bound to happen again in future.'
- Errors of judgement – as you become older and get to a more senior level, you shouldn't be making so many wrong or bad decisions any more.
- An 'honest mistake' can be excused, but there is no excuse for a 'sly mistake' where dishonesty is involved.

CHAPTER 3

Brand Pretorius

FORMERLY AT TOYOTA AND MCCARTHY, CURRENTLY DIRECTOR OF COMPANIES | *Interview broadcast on 19 July 2011*

Brand was fascinated by the motor industry from an early age and made it the subject of his MCom dissertation at the University of the Orange Free State. In 1973 he joined Toyota SA, at that stage a small player, with a mere 7% share of the passenger vehicle market in South Africa. By the time he left the company, Toyota had been established as the country's market leader in the motor industry. Brand joined McCarthy in 1995, where he played a pivotal role in saving the group from bankruptcy and preserving thousands of jobs. Nowadays, Brand concentrates on mentoring young business leaders and also serves as non-executive director on the boards of several leading South African companies.

Brand's career at Toyota South Africa started in 1973, when Dr Albert Wessels was chief executive of the company. With the very small market share it had at the time, Toyota wasn't regarded as a serious player in the local motor market. Moreover, it was an era when anything from Japan was still viewed as cheap and unreliable. Our conversation began with those first few years at Toyota under Wessels.

Brand's admiration for Wessels was palpable. 'I remember the privilege I had of working under a visionary leader like Dr Albert Wessels, of being able to learn from him. He inspired me, and, as such, he naturally played a huge role in my career and in my life. I recall the excitement of building the Toyota brand, of the development and implementation of the integrated marketing plan.' Brand elaborated on the thrilling times as they saw Toyota progress and eventually become a market leader. With that achieved, they began talking about sustainability and 'shifted the focus more to customer satisfaction'. Looking back on all the work they did there, and 'of course the inspiration I got from working with a wonderful team', he sums up the experience as 'a period where everything kept going right'. ('Everything keeps going right' was also the Toyota slogan at the time.)

Brand was with Toyota for 22 years. But, one December holiday, he decided to compile a formal document, addressed to himself, which he called 'A Case for Change'. Anyone who spends some time in Brand's company will be struck by his painstaking thoroughness; everything is analysed rationally, to the finest detail. This was also the approach he took as he contemplated his future, weighing up the advantages and disadvantages of moving to the McCarthy motor retail group. It might sound strange to do a presentation to oneself by way of a formal document, but the way he explained it was in keeping with his trademark logic. 'Keeping in mind all the joy and success I had been privileged to experience at Toyota, I told myself that, after 22 years, I would like to broaden my horizons, learn something new.'

The retail side of the motor industry had always interested him, and, besides, there was 'a personal side to this whole equation'. He wanted to restore some balance to his life and to devote more time to his family. Hence the opportunity at McCarthy attracted Brand 'because I believed that I would learn new things, experience a career rebirth of sorts, and at the same time be able to maintain a better work/life balance'.

The upshot was that he joined McCarthy, but what the move brought him was far from the goal of the more balanced life he had set in 'A Case for Change' – on the contrary, it flew in the face of his plan. After a stint as chief executive of the motor business, Brand was appointed chief executive of the group and found himself at the helm of a large bankrupt business. I asked him what his approach was in attempting to get the group back on its feet and save about 15 000 jobs. In Brand's view, accepting responsibility is a fundamental principle of leadership. 'There were many innocent victims involved in the technical insolvency of McCarthy, because the employees were not to blame for McCarthy's problems.' McCarthy was a diversified group with extensive interests in the furniture trade and in clothing, he explains, and the problems had originated on this 'non-motor side of the business' as a result of massive write-offs of bad debt. 'So I felt that I had the responsibility to look after the shareholders' interests, but primarily I was concerned about the people who would be the innocent victims.'

He recalls how he and his team worked around the clock to develop a turnaround strategy and tried their utmost to retain their excellent and talented employees. 'Of course, there was only one way this could be done: going to the banks, literally on our knees, and pleading with them to recapitalise the group.' Brand says he did this 'with conviction, for my people and because I believed it to be very likely that we could save the group. The motor retail business was a quality business, and that was the case I presented to the banks.' He was grateful that the banks were prepared to recapitalise McCarthy, thereby saving many thousands of jobs.

With the ship stabilised, McCarthy's motor business was sold to the industrial group Bidvest and Brand stayed on as chief executive for seven years. I wanted to know what it was like for him to work within a totally different culture and under the Bidvest chief executive Brian Joffe. Brand describes the Bidvest culture as very entrepreneurial and highly results-driven, nimble and fast-moving, with very clear accountability. 'Growth is part of the religion of Bidvest', which is encapsulated in what has become a kind of a slogan of theirs: 'ROFE for Joffe' (short for 'return on funds employed'). This 'tough culture' was a good training school for him: 'In certain respects a relentless emphasis on results, but I gained valuable experience from it.'

With Brand now serving on the boards of various companies and organisations and focusing on mentoring young business leaders, how does he view leadership? In his opinion, 'leadership has nothing to do with authority, position or self-importance. The days of autocratic bosses are past.' His philosophy is that leaders should have 'the courage to walk in front, to give direction'. Leaders have to set the best example, because it is through one's example that one inspires others. 'They have to earn their influence and the respect and trust of their people. There is no short cut. And leaders also need to have the ability to touch the hearts of their people, which can be achieved only by being willing to serve them. That, in essence, is my leadership approach.'

Nowadays, he has a little more time to himself than when he still occupied executive positions. When I ask him how he spends it, Brand singles out 'virtually rediscovering my family' as his first priority. His second is to learn new things and also to serve more; the non-executive directorships he has accepted are all outside the motor industry, and much of his time is devoted to community projects. He is motivated by the urge 'to try and make a difference in South Africa, because we live in a country where the needs are almost overwhelming and where

I believe all of us have a responsibility to help ensure that tomorrow is going to be better than today'.

What emerged clearly during the conversation with Brand is the absolute sincerity and honesty with which he approaches everything, including the interview. Maybe that is why the easier life he envisaged in 'A Case for Change' was always destined to take a back seat to his sense of duty and his commitment to making a difference.

ADVICE TO YOUNG PEOPLE

- Make sure that you know from early on what your passion is.
- Develop your personal dream for the future, 'a dream of what you want to be, what you want to achieve'.
- Develop a solid foundation when it comes to principles and values. 'You have to identify what those principles and values are, and then, of course, strive to live up to them to the best of your ability.'
- In your work, your focus should be on excellent results. 'Many young people fall into the trap of placing more emphasis on their career ambitions than on their results.'
- Hard work and perseverance are both key success factors. You should simply put your shoulder to the wheel and do your absolute best.

CHAPTER 4

Bernard Swanepoel

FORMERLY AT HARMONY, CHIEF EXECUTIVE OF THE VILLAGE MAIN
REEF MINING GROUP | *Interview broadcast on 26 July 2011*

(GALLO IMAGES)

Bernard started out at the Grootvlei gold mine as an 18-year-old junior mineworker. He obtained a degree in Mining Engineering from the University of Pretoria, to which he later added a BCom (Hons) degree through part-time study. After a number of years in the gold-mining industry he joined Harmony, a struggling single-operation gold mine. For 12 years he led the team that saw Harmony grow into the world's fifth-largest gold-mining group, with a market value of about R33 billion. Bernard is currently co-owner and chief executive of the JSE-listed Village Main Reef mining group.

Bernard's passion for mining was clear from the outset. Not many people would urge youngsters to spend their gap year down a mine, but, in his view, this is an option that could be made attractive to school leavers!

Accordingly, I began the interview by taking us back to the 18-year-old Bernard, who started his career as a junior mineworker at the Grootvlei mine. Why was it important to him to start at the bottom? Partly it was 'out of necessity', says Bernard, because it provided a way to obtain a bursary for university studies. But, looking back today, he also reckons that it equipped him with the necessary experience. 'It formed part of those 10 000 hours of apprenticeship that are so vital.'

Bernard qualified as a mining engineer at the University of Pretoria and later obtained a BCom (Hons) in Financial Management through part-time study. Nowadays, he remarks, a more typical combination would probably be to do an MBA after an engineering degree, but 'when you're in the process of successfully building your career' in the mining industry you can't take time off for full-time studying. 'I decided to improve my financial knowledge on a part-time basis, and I have to say, as a businessman, at the end of the day, the financial aspect of one's skills is very important.'

The young Bernard joined the Beatrix gold mine, part of the Gencor Group, and the feat of transforming this mine into the lowest-cost gold producer in the country is attributed to him. He comments modestly that 'he was just the lucky guy who was given an opportunity at a young age'. Peter Robinson, the decision-maker within Gencor at the time, 'believed in young people'. Bernard also emphasises the vital role played by the team he found at Beatrix, people like Ferdi Dippenaar and Neal Froneman. 'All I had to say was, "Guys, we're the 50th-cheapest producer in the country; surely we want to be the lowest-cost producer", and, with the help of that team and of the 5 000 workers, it wasn't so difficult to achieve.'

After two years as general manager at Beatrix, he exchanged a successful career at a big mining company for the role of managing director of the much smaller and marginal Harmony mine. In response to my question about the reasons behind this decision, Bernard explains that, despite the support he enjoyed at Gencor, it was still not possible for him 'to go and do exactly what I believed the industry needed'. From what he knew of Harmony, it was 'a mine whose situation was so desperate that we would be allowed to do some things differently'. Randgold (owners of Harmony) had been taken over by people such as Roger Kebble and Peter Flack at the time, 'and everything they said sounded to me like what the industry needed. Let's start at the top, change the industry from the top downwards. It was a rather different recipe, so when Roger Kebble phoned and said he wanted to talk to me, I told him I had been waiting for his call, and the rest is history.'

In the 12 years that followed, and after a string of acquisitions, Bernard grew the single-operation Harmony mine, with a value of R1.5 billion, to the world's fifth-largest gold-mining group, with a value of about R33 billion. When he looks back on that era, what did Harmony do right? As Bernard puts it, Harmony had to become productive out of sheer necessity, because it was a low-grade mine. As all the high-grade ore had already been mined, Harmony's production costs per ton were the lowest in the industry. 'With the help of Graham Briggs, who now manages Harmony, and a few other people, we perhaps added a bit of discipline to the management of the ore body. In other words, low costs per ton are good, but you also have to mine the right tons at the right grade.' As a result of Anglo Gold's strategy at the time of selling mines that no longer fitted into their core operations, there were many mines available that, according to Bernard, 'needed exactly that recipe'. In the end, he says, it was 'such a simple recipe that, 15 transactions later, we had become a big mining company'.

This recipe of making marginal mines profitable through more efficient cost management was later dubbed 'the Harmony way', a term he attributes to Neal Froneman, who currently heads Sibanye Gold. According to Bernard, it was so successful 'that the biggest challenge was always to try and explain to an American investor why everyone wasn't doing it'.

Today Bernard is co-owner and chief executive of the Village Main Reef group. When I ask him about his plans for Village, he says it is still the basic recipe of taking over a mine that is deemed cheap because it is not worth much, 'and then doing a few things differently' so that its value increases. 'I don't even want to say running it in a smarter or cleverer way; that sounds too arrogant. We just do it in a different way.' He explains that, in the case of Harmony, 'we continued to own the mines and that's why they became more profitable. At Village we say we're going to apply the same recipe – it doesn't only work for gold. In fact, I think there are fantastic opportunities in platinum, and when we have done what we can, we want to hand over the mine to whoever wants to become the next owner. In every kind of deal, we make sure that the community is involved. We ensure that the workers have ownership and that management not only manages but also has ownership, and then we can own the mine from where it costs R1 to where it might be worth R100 million.'

Reflecting on his career, Bernard remarks that he landed in mining by chance, and once again stresses the value of starting at the bottom. In his view, 'fate probably determined my career more than I did', and he benefited from the help of people who 'looked after me fantastically' at the right times. In retrospect, he believes that 'when it would have been very easy to go to Australia, or become a mining analyst, or go into banking, probably the smartest thing I did was just to grit my teeth, go underground and do my apprenticeship properly'. Not that he thinks you can manage a company only if you started at the bottom, 'but when you have come up through the ranks it's just a big advantage. I worked in the time office. I was an onsetter, the person in charge of winding operations underground. I drilled and I blasted. Today I realise what the full value of that practical experience is.'

As someone who is himself a beneficiary of opportunities granted to him at a young age, Bernard is passionate about young people and believes that 'if you fail to create opportunities for people, you're not exploiting your chief asset'. He says he is extremely proud of some of the young people with whom he has worked, 'and today I phone them for advice'. Bernard refers to Jan Nelson of Pan African Resources as an example: 'Behind his back I call him one of my success stories, but of course I can never claim that in his presence because he is his own success story.'

According to Bernard, Harmony was at one stage renowned for leading the way in transformation and providing opportunities to young people of all races and backgrounds. He reckons 'the biggest tragedy of our country is that young people can't find jobs nowadays', and sees it as a challenge that the mining industry should be made attractive to them again. Eighteen-year-olds 'should want to put their university studies on hold for a year because they are keen to go and work in a mine. It will be a fantastic future if we can manage to do that again.'

I wanted to get the views of a successful mining entrepreneur, someone well versed in all facets of mining and now also an owner of mining assets, on the state's role in mining and also whether he considers the debate on this topic a healthy one. Firstly, this debate will stay with us, says Bernard, and, secondly, 'it is perhaps a legitimate debate'. Referring to the global cycles with regard to the role of the state, nationalisation and privatisation, he says that 'we are today one of the few countries where this is being debated, but there is almost no country in the world where nationalisation hasn't happened at some or other time'. The world is at present 'highly conscious of the scarcity of natural resources, and when something is scarce, one's government starts taking an interest on behalf of the people of the country. So, I believe it's healthy to have this debate. We need to find the balance where the people of the country receive the appropriate share of the pie.'

In South Africa, mineral rights already belong to the state, 'so they have been nationalised'. But 'the person who brings the capital should get a sound, risk-adjusted return on his capital'. Bernard says that, as an investor, he will not invest in a gold mine if he is not going to be adequately rewarded for his risk. If Village establish a company and are unsure of whether they will be able to run the mine for 25 years, 'we'll never invest the R10 billion it takes to run a mine'. As someone who is not an advocate of state ownership, Bernard declares, he is of the view that 'we stopped a bit too soon with privatisation' in South Africa, and that 'our state-owned entities are not examples of successful organisations'. Which is a pity, he adds, 'because if they were successful companies, we could have had a useful debate. Given that it is not the case, just about all that we as capitalists can say is, "Do you want to run our mines like you are running our state-owned entities, or our airline?" Surely not. While it should actually have been a healthy debate about which works best, a successful state-owned organisation as opposed to a successful privately owned organisation.' But he remains hopeful that we will have a healthy debate on this topic in future.

Bernard did not choose mining as a career; mining chose him, and his love for the industry was infectious throughout the interview. His faith in the ability of young people stands out as clearly as his passion for mining – even when he is talking about the role of the state. If someone like Bernard is still positive about mining, one has to pay attention.

BERNARD'S SUMMARY OF 'THE HARMONY WAY'

- Harmony was serious about cutting costs: 'absolutely no unnecessary expenses were incurred'.
- 'We used to joke and say that our roads have potholes, but our ore body contains no potholes.'
- 'We tried to spend the money in the right place.'
- The team believed from the outset that they wouldn't succeed unless they could 'sort out the working relationship' with their workers. 'There was a time when the country was going through serious transformation, there was a time when the trade unions knew they could bring a mine to a standstill if they wanted to, and we had to manage all those relationships and get the workers on our side.'

CHAPTER 5

Mardia van der Walt-Korsten

MANAGING DIRECTOR OF T-SYSTEMS SOUTH AFRICA

Interview broadcast on 2 August 2011

Mardia obtained an MA in Clinical Psychology from the University of Stellenbosch and worked in human resource management. In 1998 she joined T-Systems South Africa, a global IT services and consulting company that is a subsidiary of Deutsche Telekom. In 2005 Mardia was appointed as the acting chief executive for T-Systems South Africa, the first woman ever to hold this position, and officially became managing director a year later. Under her leadership, the business was turned around and the annual turnover increased from R650 million to R3 billion in five years. Mardia was named as South Africa's Businesswoman of the Year in 2008. (In 2012 she was appointed head of T-Systems' newly formed Africa region and chairperson of the board of T-Systems South Africa.)

On the face of it, it seems strange that the head of an information and communications technology (ITC) company holds a master's degree in psychology instead of a computer science or business degree. I began the interview by asking Mardia what her psychology background had contributed to her success. 'I believe it helps me to understand people to an extent,' she says, but, on her appointment as chief executive, her unorthodox background raised quite a few eyebrows. 'The first reaction of many people was, how can you run a technology company if you don't have a directly technical background?' What she will always remember, Mardia adds, is how her ten-year-old son responded when she tried to explain to him what kind of work T-Systems does. When he heard that his mother had been put in charge of this company, he exclaimed: 'How can they give you such a job? You don't know anything about computers!'

In 1998 she joined T-Systems and in 2005 she was appointed as the first female chief executive within this multinational group. Mardia confesses that her appointment came as 'a very big surprise'. She had been away on maternity leave for a few months after the birth of her third child, and had assumed that she would be returning to her old position. On her return, however, the then CEO had a discussion with her, saying that they had 'big problems with sales and where we were in the market at that stage'; he needed someone to turn the situation around, to look differently at the business and 'to put the company on a truly different growth path'.

As we started focusing more on Mardia's business career, the value of her knowledge of human nature and of her specific application of these insights increasingly came to the fore. When Mardia took over the reins, the annual turnover was R650 million; the target of R1 billion in turnover was reached in 2008, and R3 billion was achieved in 2010. To what does she attribute this growth? The major issue when it comes to the implementation of a strategy, she says, is that you have to know yourself extremely well. 'You have to be sure of what you know, but it is especially important to know what your knowledge gaps are.' Accordingly, she put together a team of people who were, in her view, 'absolute experts in their field' and together they 'put a plan on the table'. They wanted to get all 600 of the company's employees enthusiastic about the goal, 'and the goal was big enough to make us all scared enough and really passionate about achieving it'. It was a matter of 'getting every single person in the company to understand what it was that he or she had to do every day in order to reach that goal'.

Their business grew from 600 to 2 700 employees. How does one implement a strategy in such a big group? The challenge, in her view, is that every employee should understand what the strategy means in terms of their interaction with customers and their daily jobs. 'So we set the overall goal for ourselves that we wanted to achieve something more. We wanted to do something that has meaning.' Referring to Guy Kawasaki's concept of 'making meaning', Mardia notes that Kawasaki says if you focus on making meaning in your company, you will probably make money anyway. 'There is so much arrogance in different kinds of businesses, especially once you start to become successful, and to me the important thing was to say that we are ordinary people, ordinary South Africans who are IT specialists, HR specialists, financial specialists, and we want to make magic.'

She has strong views on the merits of a culture of decision-making that allows for mistakes, believing that 'it is ten times worse to do nothing'. By avoiding decisions and doing nothing you won't make mistakes, but you won't achieve anything either. 'Hence I prefer that people take the risk, make a decision and embark on something. We would rather make a mistake, learn from it and grow – I believe this culture has been one of our successes.'

Mardia was named South Africa's Businesswoman of the Year in 2008. In one of her speeches she remarked that women are sometimes more inclined to ask for, and to accept, advice, and that this attribute is an advantage to them in the business world. When I ask her about this observation, Mardia says that while the statement may be a generalisation, it has 'a bit to do with ego'. The IT environment is still a fairly male-centred world. 'I tend to joke a bit with them by saying that men have more trouble with this ego thing. Obviously not all women are ego-free, but I think if you can admit that you don't know everything, you must feel reasonably good about where you are and who you are. To me, that is the art of a company that has a learning culture and an environment that says we're not perfect.' Mardia believes that 'that ability to communicate with another person, of being able to really hear and really listen, not just listening to what you would like to hear', is 'a tremendous advantage' for T-Systems.

She adds that women generally adapt more easily to changing circumstances, which, in her view, is related to 'the different roles we often have to play'. In her own case, she is a mother of three sons. Raising children is 'an unpredictable process', with different personalities, time schedules and things that need to be done. 'You have this sense that you have to make all these things happen and you need to be able to give equal attention to everyone.'

The focus on people and the need to understand them ran like a thread through the interview. I wanted to broaden the topic a bit and asked Mardia for her views on capitalism and the greed that often accompanies deals. In her opinion, the whole period of the financial crisis of 2008 'basically came down to greed'. At the time, the T-Systems team thought hard about what had really happened. 'What are companies doing, and what is it really about? For me, it always comes back to the question of meaning: why do we exist?' If one looks at T-Systems as an ITC company, for instance, 'is our only purpose to support and fix computer systems, to enable people to communicate?'

Mardia believes one should be able to connect a company's reason for existence to 'a bigger purpose, a bigger dream'. Once they got close to the achievement of a R3-billion company, she says, they 'started walking a road' where they said: 'But what comes next? Is our goal now just going to be to become bigger? Make more money?' Obviously T-Systems is there to make money for the shareholders and to benefit the people in the organisation. Profitability is essential, but, to them, it is ultimately about moving from success to significance.

To Mardia, this relates to the concept of capitalism 'with a soul', where you say that, of course, making money is part of the goal. 'But when you are on that road of moving from success to significance, it's about something more than just that.' At T-Systems they told themselves: 'We will know we are significant when we are the best for the people who work for us and the best for our customers, and within the context of what is the best for South Africa – not the best in the country, or the biggest in the country. "Best in" is not a goal for me, but "best for", and that's a total emphasis shift.' It is significant, she adds, when you hear the stories of people from, say, rural villages who are now working in a highly specialised IT environment. 'Then you know that you have changed people's lives, and for me that is what it's really about.'

Mardia sees the same debate when it comes to the issue of leadership. She emphasises that one of a leader's goals should be to make profit, because that is a basic part of being in business. To her, business is not in conflict with morality. What is hard, however, is to make business work in a way that is consistent with morality and to live those principles. It is easy to say 'we want this capitalism with a soul, or a less greedy capitalism', she admits, but truly putting it into practice is a very long process. She would never claim that they have already achieved it at T-Systems, Mardia says, because 'one works with people' and they are themselves still in the process of reflecting on what it really means to do business ethically in a context of profit and competition. She explains that it is an ongoing process for them and 'a journey where we are constantly debating about it, and to me that is the beginning. The beginning is to turn it into a conversation where you get people to at least start thinking and asking questions about it, and then hopefully to arrive one day at the answer as to what it really means.'

What distinguished this interview from the others is that the human being featured much more prominently. When talking about strategy and company success, Mardia constantly returns to the individual person within the company and how every individual has to be part of the plan. This is where her psychology background gives her an advantage over the technical or financial specialists. I am also convinced of the need for people with a humanities or social science background to play a greater role in the debates about the sharp end of capitalism; we shouldn't be leaving it up to those with a purely 'hard' business orientation to determine the rules of the game on their own.

CORE PURPOSE OF A LEADER

- To have hope that you are going to reach your goal, that you are going to get out of the mess in which you find yourself at present, that your plans will be successful, whatever your circumstances may be.
- To give other people hope.
- To have empathy with your colleagues and to get everyone to believe that goals are attainable.

ADVICE TO A YOUNG WOMAN IN THE BUSINESS WORLD

- Become an expert in your field.
- Whatever you are given to do, or find to do on your own, do it as well as you can, and better than anybody else.
- Be authentic. Be yourself, and don't try to emulate a male role model.

CHAPTER 6

Dr Johan van Zyl

CHIEF EXECUTIVE OF TOYOTA SA

Interview broadcast on 9 August 2011

Johan was a professor of Marketing at the former Potchefstroom University (where he had also obtained his doctorate) when he decided, in 1993, to exchange academic life for a senior position at Toyota SA. Today he is chief executive of Toyota SA, a company with about 8 000 employees and an annual turnover of R50 billion. Out of respect for the holding company, he learned to read and speak Japanese. In 2009, Johan was appointed to the position of managing officer in the top management structure of the Toyota Motor Corporation of Japan, one of only five non-Japanese to have been appointed at this level in the history of the company. In addition to offices in Johannesburg and Port Elizabeth, he runs a full-time office in Tokyo.

As Johan had been a professor at the former Potchefstroom University (today part of North-West University) and also obtained most of his degrees with distinction, it seemed appropriate to start our conversation by asking his opinion on the value of a strong academic background for career success. Johan reckons that, if you want to empower people, 'your first focus should be on training and academic background, which is not to say that it has to be a degree'. He happens to believe that a strong academic background is important, 'but it doesn't guarantee success'. According to Johan, universities should focus more on teaching people how to think and less on trying to coach them. 'We here in the business world will teach them how to do specific things through in-service training, but we're looking for people who can really think differently, who can be innovative, but who are also able to understand broader concepts.'

Toyota is a phenomenally successful company, both globally and in South Africa. When I ask Johan about the history of Toyota SA and the role of its founder, Dr Albert Wessels, he points out that this is 'a remarkable success story that South Africans should look at. It's a kind of model for our future.' Dr Wessels, an entrepreneur, started the company as a small enterprise in 1961 by importing ten vehicles. And when you tell people that he started the business at the age of 55, Johan adds, 'they can't believe it', because at 55 most of us start planning our retirement. From its humble beginnings, Toyota had grown by 1980 to become the local market leader. Johan describes the foundation laid by Dr Wessels, and later also by his son Bert Wessels and daughter Elizabeth Bradley, as a company that was highly value-oriented, with a strong culture that was modelled on Toyota Japan's approach.

Another striking similarity between Toyota SA and the Japanese holding company is the strong family substructure, and Johan still refers to Toyota SA as 'a family'. When they talk of the 'Toyota family', he explains, it obviously comprises Toyota SA itself, but also their dealer network, their suppliers, and everyone who has an interest in the company. 'I always say that a family doesn't get divorced. We might murder each other, but we won't divorce. We are connected to each other. We look after each other. We care about each other. We work together to bring about a better future for all of us, and that's where the notion of the Toyota family comes from.' And, like Toyota in Japan, a family business that was started by the Toyoda family, Toyota in South Africa is a family business that was started by the Wessels family.

Having to manage crises is an unavoidable part of the motor market, whether it is a matter of models that have to be recalled or of faulty parts. How does Johan deal with such crises? 'The first thing you shouldn't do,' he says, 'is get into a panic. I believe one just has to take a deep breath and think carefully about what really happened.' In his experience, however, every crisis is also a good learning opportunity, a chance to understand. He uses the example of the March 2011 tsunami in Japan as 'another of those things that turned out to be a tremendous learning opportunity for us as far as risk management and risk prevention are concerned. The impact of such a massive natural disaster on your organisation – when you tell people it might happen, they don't consider it likely, but what do you do the day it actually happens? But a crisis is a wonderful opportunity. People always think it sounds strange when you say that, but if you really think about it … if you haven't yet had a crisis, you haven't learned.'

Here is a South African who holds the distinction of serving on the executive board of the Toyota Motor Corporation of Japan, one of only five non-Japanese who have reached this level – and this in one of the world's biggest and most successful companies. Given his academic and corporate experience, what are Johan's views on business leadership? He declares frankly that he dislikes the notion of 'hero managers' or 'hero leaders'. 'To my mind, you should just be yourself. The team is all-important. You have to get a team to really believe in, understand and contribute to that which we want to achieve, and then work with absolute commitment to achieve it in practice.' And when the goal is reached, 'it's not a victory for an individual; it's a victory for the team. That's just part of the Toyota culture, the way we always work.' They like people with creativity and innovative ideas and are keen to draw them into their team, 'but what it's ultimately about in a business is how your team performs'. It's almost like sport, Johan says. 'I have a simple philosophy. You can make a mistake once and then you have to learn from it. We're constantly learning.'

What has always struck me about Toyota is how they manage to come across as South African, as if it were a genuinely homegrown brand. Johan replies with a smile: 'But it is!' They have always positioned Toyota as a truly South African company, he says, also because of the history of the company in the country. They try to convey this in their communication, for instance, by incorporating typical South African humour in their advertisements. If we want to appeal to local customers, Johan explains, 'we have to build that link between the customer's culture and our product culture'.

After the interview, I kept thinking about the magnitude of Johan's achievement in becoming part of a multinational company's global management team. Toyota may be a household name among South Africans, but not many of them know that the head of Toyota South Africa is also a world leader in the international motor industry.

TOYOTA'S KEY BUILDING BLOCKS FOR SUCCESS

- **Respect for people** – This principle requires one to respect other people's opinions, their property, their feelings and their work. 'All work should be respected. All people who work should be respected. The guy who makes the tea should be respected too, and he should be given the same kind of respect that is due to the head of the company, because he is a human being, he provides a service, he makes a contribution, and this is what respect for people is all about.'

- ***Kaizen*, or continuous improvement** – In Japanese thinking, no process can ever be declared perfect, where you can say you are satisfied with what you have achieved. They always say: 'That which we have achieved now was done well, but how are we going to improve on it?'

ADVICE TO PEOPLE AT THE START OF THEIR CAREERS

- Take your studies seriously and choose something that you would really like to do – success cannot be measured only by money. 'For me, success is measured by whether you can truly fulfil yourself and whether you enjoy what you do. I can imagine nothing worse than going to work every day and doing something that you don't enjoy.'
- Start with enthusiasm, work with enthusiasm and put in the time. We have brilliant human material in South Africa, and if you want to be an entrepreneur start immediately. Don't wait.

CHAPTER 7

Jannie Mouton

NON-EXECUTIVE CHAIRMAN OF THE PSG GROUP

Interview broadcast on 16 August 2011

(GALLO IMAGES)

Jannie hails from Carnarvon in the Karoo. His father was an entrepreneur, a teacher who later started a shop in the town. As a child, Jannie had to listen to share prices on the radio and then discuss market trends and their share investments with his father. In his primary-school days he was already familiar with listed companies and what they did. After studying at Stellenbosch University and qualifying as a chartered accountant, Jannie spent some time in the corporate world and then co-founded the JSE broking firm SMK, from which he was later fired by his fellow directors. As an unemployed 50-year-old, Jannie started the PSG Group, which by 2012 had grown into a business empire with a market value exceeding R12 billion. He is currently non-executive chairman of the group.

After seven years at Federale Volksbeleggings as a chartered accountant, the 35-year-old Jannie took a leap into entrepreneurship and co-founded SMK, a JSE broking firm, with two friends. He had to approach his mother and his wife for loans to scrape together his capital contribution of R50 000. SMK was a very successful business, but on 5 August 1995 the bottom was knocked out of Jannie's world. He had dropped the children at school and drove to work as usual, with no inkling of what awaited him at the office. Two hours later, his partners summarily sacked him from his position as managing director.

This sudden dismissal was 'probably the turning point in my life', Jannie says, 'because it wasn't only a surprise; it was a shock and a humiliation. You're worried about the future, and you're a bit embittered as well. You're angry.' After a month or two of agonising, however, 'I realised that I simply had to turn my head around and carry on with my life.'

At the age of almost 50 he had been a respected businessman heading a successful firm, and this setback clearly hit him hard. But Jannie did not nurse his wounds and grudges for too long; he devoted the free time he had at his disposal to reading, thinking and planning. He submitted himself to the discipline of getting dressed neatly every day, 'so that I at least looked as if I'm clocking in at eight', and kept himself busy in his office at home by reading business and motivational books, which he summarised. 'My wife typed the summaries for me and gradually I started gaining clarity on what I wanted to do in life. I wrote this down too, put it on my desk and looked at it every day, and in that way I developed a plan.'

In 1995 he started a business that would later become the PSG Group, an investment holding company which, in 2012, consisted of 42 underlying investments operating across industries that include financial services, banking, private equity, agriculture and education. To put the success of the group into perspective: if you had invested

R100 000 in PAG shares in 1995, the year Jannie bought the listed company PAG (which would later become the PSG Group), this investment would have been worth more than R100 million in 2012. He managed to take the group from a market value of R7 million to a value of more than R12 billion in 2012 – in about 17 years.

Among the highlights on the road of this financial success story are the establishment and listing of Capitec Bank, the listed agricultural investment company Zeder, the recently listed Curro private-school group, and the successful PSG Konsult financial-advice businesses.

The PSG Group was started in the post-1994 South Africa, and I wanted to get Jannie's opinion on the current business environment and the country's future. Jannie says there is no doubt in his mind: 'The opportunities are in South Africa. As I often tell people, we wouldn't have stood a chance trying to start something like Capitec in Europe. Everything has already been done there, in a manner of speaking. So, this country has a multitude of opportunities. Enormous opportunities.' As an example, he refers to Thembeka, a 51% black-owned and -controlled company that is part of PSG: it started with nothing and is now worth in excess of R1 billion. Every now and again he and his team do get a bit worried about issues like the nationalisation of banks and mines, he admits, 'but I don't think the risk is so great. A country of opportunities.'

PSG has a tiny head office in Stellenbosch; you can count the staff members on your fingers. When I ask Jannie why he chose to station himself there, he traces this decision back to his abrupt departure from SMK. He confesses that he has realised he has a bit of a problem, too. 'Maybe it's aggression, driving people too hard, impatience. That's why I'm now sitting here in Stellenbosch, and all the operations are in other places.' It is something to which he has given much thought: 'You have to give people freedom within a clearly defined framework.'

What struck me during our conversation is that Jannie is actually practising his hobby (as he says, 'I love coming to the office') and intends keeping up this hobby for many years to come. His mentor, Warren Buffett, is 16 years older than Jannie, and 'he's still doing well'. After the interview, we spoke about the criticism he incurred as a result of his son Piet succeeding him as chief executive. His justification of this decision is simple – the wealth of the Mouton family is vested in PSG shares, therefore it is in his interest to appoint the best person to look after the family assets. And to this one can add that Jannie has never sold a single PSG share.

MANAGEMENT POINTS

- **Ultimate empowerment** – Give people the freedom to take decisions, even if they make mistakes, but within an agreed-upon, clearly defined framework and on the understanding that they have to be honest even if things are not going well.
- **A stake in the business** – Senior management should own a direct stake in the respective businesses, because it motivates them to 'go that extra step'.
- **Listed subsidiaries** – Subsidiaries should be listed so that results have to be explained to shareholders and the media. 'Where would one run the best 100-metre race: in front of the grandstand under the floodlights, or behind it in the dark?'
- **Annual growth conference** – PSG believes that all the decision-makers should get together at the beginning of the year to discuss growth and look at internal as well as external opportunities.

ADVICE TO YOUNG PEOPLE ABOUT ENTREPRENEURSHIP

- 'No one should think that success comes for free' – study, read and first get some work experience in your discipline.

- Draw up a plan and discuss it with other people, but it should be a plan that you believe you can realise.
- 'At some stage you have to swap the security of a salaried job for a bit of risk, but if your ducks are in a row as far as your planning is concerned, nothing holds you back.'

CHAPTER 8

Chris Venter

CHIEF EXECUTIVE OF AFGRI

Interview broadcast on 23 August 2011

After completing a BA degree in Theology at the University of Pretoria, Chris changed tack and obtained an MBA degree. He opted for a career in banking, which included a stint of nearly three years in New York while working for Absa Corporate and Merchant Bank. In 2006 he joined the AFGRI Group as managing director of AFGRI Financial Services and Insurance. Chris was appointed as chief executive of the group in 2008.

A head of an agricultural company with a degree in Theology is not quite what you would expect – until you talk to Chris. In the course of the interview it becomes clear that his faith plays a major role in his life, especially when it comes to his desire to make a difference in people's lives.

I was curious about Chris's decision to do an MBA after having first studied theology. As he explains it, people have always been close his heart and his faith is also of great importance to him. Hence he always wanted to get involved in a field where he could work with people and also make an impact. 'I discovered very quickly that I could actually make a bigger impact in the business world, and that is basically the reason why I set out to obtain an MBA.'

After his studies, Chris embarked on a career in banking, which included nearly three years in New York. What did he gain from this international experience that, in his view, contributed to his later success? Chris describes it as 'extremely important' and regards the time he spent in New York as having been 'really an enormous advantage' to him. One of the benefits he singles out is that 'the American way of looking at business is the norm': everything is big and their way of negotiating is very specific, almost aggressive, 'yet one learns from it'. Of course, he adds, it was more than just a business experience: 'It's almost as if you learn something in your essence, your character, that you won't necessarily learn if you stay only in South Africa.'

In Chris's case, his international exposure was beneficial to his career; would he encourage young people to grasp opportunities to gain international experience? Definitely, he says, especially from a cultural angle. He believes that, in a country like South Africa, with so many different cultural groups, 'the more cultures and the more business cultures you can experience, the bigger the advantage will be for you in the business world because you learn something from that'. When you sit around a negotiating table, he says, your perceptions of the people you are dealing with are often blinkered. What you learn from such an exposure to other cultures is that there are other perceptions, 'and very often it's just the way of looking at a specific transaction that is different and not necessarily a matter of the people being negative. I would almost say that, from a transaction viewpoint, one learns an enormous amount about the different cultural groups.' To experience this cultural diversity in business is something that he would recommend to any young person.

With many South Africans choosing to build their future in other countries, why did Chris and his wife decide to return to South Africa? According to Chris, they did not go abroad with the intention of staying there. 'We had the opportunity to emigrate and stay longer, and we thought deeply about it. It was a long process of prayer, but we are Africans deep down and we wanted to return. We are part of Africa. We want to be in Africa. We want to make a difference here, or an impact here, and we never felt like leaving the country for good.'

Shortly after his return to South Africa, Chris left the banking sector for a position at the agricultural and food company AFGRI. At first glance this seems like an unusual move, yet there were similarities between his old and his new career. As Chris explains it, he was approached by AFGRI to focus primarily on their financial services division, and initially he managed that part of the business. In his banking career he had been involved in international finance and had had the opportunity of financing commodities, including food commodities. 'So the move to an agricultural company was still in the food industry, still related to food commodities.'

When Chris was appointed as chief executive of the AFGRI Group in 2008, he immediately embarked on a restructuring of the entire business. At the core of the process was the focus on what he calls the grain value chain. I wanted to know more about the philosophy behind this strategy. Chris says he believes that every company has a specific DNA; if a company wants to be successful, 'you should know what your DNA is and then protect and grow that DNA as far as possible'. When he looks back on AFGRI's 90-year history, 'AFGRI's DNA is grain and grain management and the use thereof'. So when it came to their restructuring, he said that this was what they had to go back to: 'We should nurture the DNA and build on it, and of course at the same time also know where we are heading. In other words, the vision should be constructed on that DNA.'

AFGRI is one of the country's biggest agricultural companies, with between 8 000 and 10 000 farmers as customers. If one looks at poverty and food scarcity in Africa, what does Chris consider South Africa's role to be in solving these problems? He is 'convinced that there are solutions in Africa specifically', with companies like theirs playing a part in developing such solutions. From his experience, South African farmers can have an impact in Africa through the transfer of skills, and 'we really need to take the trouble' to transfer that expertise. His passion and his focus in the future, he says, 'is to go and have an impact and to see what are the opportunities that we as an agricultural company can exploit together with the farmers in other African countries'.

In response to my question as to what he regards as the major challenges facing South African farmers. Chris focuses primarily on 'the calls for nationalisation' and issues around land protection and land ownership. Not that he sees these debates as being necessarily only negative, 'because there is a history that needs to be taken into account'. What should be done, in his view, 'is to work with the farmers and look at the solutions one can offer them'. He refers in this regard to many other African countries where land can be leased and used on a 99-year basis. Chris stresses that he's not necessarily advocating such an approach as a solution: 'All I'm saying is that there should be a proactive rapprochement on the part of farmers, on the part of agricultural companies and of course the industry players, to sit down with the government and see what solution we can find to the South African land ownership question.'

And what are his views on the role of technology in a modern farming operation? According to Chris, most farmers, particular the bigger ones, are increasingly using technology to their advantage. Examples from countries such as the United States and Australia demonstrate that technological innovations enable farmers to farm in smarter and cheaper ways and to reduce costs. Some South African farmers are, for instance, already using technology to ensure optimal fuel efficiency, and he reckons the impact of technology will increase more and more. Farmers cannot afford to be dismissive of technology in the future, he believes, and they should ensure that they transfer technology and knowledge to their employees.

When I ask Chris to describe his management style, he summarises it as 'an open-door policy with a somewhat autocratic approach'. An open-door policy does take up more of his time, 'but I enjoy obtaining the insights of the people at the grassroots level'. Besides, he believes that the employees 'know more than I do'; he must make sure that he is accessible so that the people who have the knowledge, and who work with the business on a daily basis, are able to talk to him. At the same time, though, he holds that, as a leader, you need to be 'a direct road indicator', which means that he doesn't believe in democracy when it comes to leadership and management. 'I believe that leadership is something inherent in you that has to be developed, and which you have to use to take people along with you in your vision and dreams.'

What comes across throughout is the connection between Chris's own interests and those of the community, be it the farmers in South Africa, people on the wrong side of food security or the AFGRI employees. Equally palpable is his urge to make a difference and a contribution. When I ask him about highlights in his career, Chris says that a highlight for him at present is having the opportunity 'to live my passion in terms of food security and hopefully to make an even greater impact on that in the future'. It is at this point that you realise that a theology background and an MBA are not such strange bedfellows after all!

CAREER ADVICE FOR YOUNG PEOPLE

- You must have integrity and let your actions be guided by it. 'As a young businessperson, one often tends to push the difficult decisions to the back and rather do the easy things.'
- You must know what you want. 'If you don't know where you are headed, you will never reach it.' What you want is 'not something rational that you can think up in your head, it's something that is in your heart – it's a passion that you have and if you work in line with it, you will definitely achieve success.'
- Be prepared to work hard if you are serious about getting ahead. 'Everything doesn't necessarily happen automatically.'
- Work 'in wisdom'.

CHAPTER 9

Louis von Zeuner

FORMER DEPUTY CHIEF EXECUTIVE OF ABSA

Interview broadcast on 30 August 2011

Louis started his career in banking in 1981 as a clerk at the Goodwood branch of the then Volkskas Bank. He completed his BEcon studies on a part-time basis while focusing on his career within the Absa Group. Louis progressed through the ranks until he eventually became deputy chief executive of Absa. In 2012, after more than 30 years' service, he exchanged his executive position for a non-executive directorship in the group. He serves on the boards of companies such as Telkom and Edcon and is involved in some of South Africa's major sports bodies at board level.

The interview with Louis was unique in several respects. He is one of the few people I talked to who had remained with the same employer from whom they had received their first salary cheque. In his case, he retired 30 years later as the boss. Also, one got the impression that Louis was available at all times. While we were organising the interview, he responded to messages regardless of the time of day. And Louis was also one of the few guests who requested me to ask him a specific question about an issue he wanted to raise.

I started our conversation at the point where a young Louis began his career at the Goodwood branch of the former Volkskas Bank in 1981. Did he ever see himself at that time as one of the bank's future bosses? Definitely not, says Louis, and his late father would probably also have responded with 'an emphatic "no"' to this question. Louis had started at the bank while continuing his studies part-time at night, and his father was firmly convinced that when a person began to earn money he would never complete his degree. Louis admits that his initial university years 'were not exactly successful', on the one hand, because he 'was no threat to the school's dux pupil on the academic side', and on the other, because his passion for sport affected his class attendance. Advancing to the upper echelons of the bank was, therefore, not something he could even have dreamt of at the time. It was rather something 'that grows within you as you get opportunities'.

It is widely believed nowadays that people should rather gain experience at different companies than stick to one employer for their entire career, and I wanted to hear Louis's opinion on this, in view of his own experience. He reckons that times have changed, and that it is harder today to have such a long career in one workplace. He also points to an international trend of big corporate organisations tending to use labour 'as and when necessary'. This could easily happen in South Africa too, which would require us to change our thinking about the current stigma that may be attached to the loss of employment. 'I think this trend will eventually spread to South Africa as well.' He often tells young people within Absa that they need to be permanently assured of their marketability. 'What is the price on your head in the outside world for the specific skills you bring? It's important that there should be a demand for your services and skills, but we also have to realise that talent must be deployable anywhere. It's good to spread your wings,' he maintains.

What did change in recent years at Louis's workplace is that Absa got a foreign controlling shareholder: the UK's Barclays Bank. How did a seasoned Absa banker experience this new shareholder? On 'the positive side', Louis singles out two aspects of the Barclays transaction. Barclays was 'not a strong retail bank player', he explains, but they were strong in corporate banking, an area in which Absa was relatively weak. Hence one of the 'easier things' about the transaction was that big job losses were not part of the deal. And because it was a 'complementary relationship', people within the organisation did not feel so threatened as far as their own positions were concerned. When it comes to the challenges presented by the new situation, Louis recalls that, in 2005, they suddenly had to work together with a company that was listed in the United Kingdom and the United States, and at once Absa was subject to international rules and regulations that did not apply to some of their competitors in South Africa. 'You often felt that you cannot really compete here because there are other regulations with which you have to comply, but I believe this will ultimately also hold long-term benefits.'

Many people reckon that South Africa's retail bank services lead the field globally in certain areas. Does Louis agree with this view? It's perhaps part of our culture that we tend to think 'if it's international it must be better than what is local', he says. What rather surprised him was that South Africa was at that stage far more advanced than Barclays in areas such as electronic banking services to the customer. He believes Absa was definitely ahead of them with regard to certain services and products, and 'at least very competitive'. Nowadays retail banks elsewhere are perhaps catching up with us faster as far as certain aspects are concerned. Louis warns against the risk of stagnating and becoming complacent: 'We should never stop thinking innovatively about our solutions.'

Absa is a banking group with more than 40 000 employees. From a leadership perspective, how does one manage so many people in a team? Louis believes that, as a leader, you should first realise that you will accomplish very little on your own; you need to have the right people around you. He feels strongly that the power of many organisations lies in their diversity. But when it comes to diversity, we should guard against labelling it as being only about colour. In Louis's view, diversity is a wider concept that also comprises differences with regard to gender and ways of thinking. So when you work 'in this team dynamic', it is very important to have people with different opinions in your group. 'We must create a climate where people not only have the right, but also the will, to express their views and to have their own opinions, so that in the end you can sit back, process the contributions of the team and take the decision that is best for the organisation.' Louis believes it is vital that leaders should always know what the organisation's vision and strategy is and whether they have people who share those collective goals and subscribe to the same value systems. What it amounts to is that 'we have to be highly adaptable in a changing environment – no single person always has the answers, or all the right answers.'

The specific issue Louis wanted to raise is the perception in some sections of our society that there are not really opportunities and a future for all in the new South Africa. While it stands to reason that this is a complex question, I was nonetheless keen to get an opinion on the subject from a banker that does considerable business with the state and is also a big employment provider. Louis believes that, notwithstanding certain aspects and realities, 'the greater goal for you and me is still to create an environment that will function normally so that our children and everybody else can benefit from a normalised environment; getting there is a process, and it's not always an easy one.' Still, he reckons that 'the opportunities do exist', and refers to his own career as an example of what he means. A born Capetonian ('and as you know, we don't easily leave the mountain'), he decided early on in his career that if he wanted to get somewhere in the bank, he had to be prepared to move around and do his stints in small towns, where he gained valuable experience. He firmly believes 'that for any individual who is committed, who works hard, who possesses the technical knowledge and skills, and who has the will to get to the top, that getting-to-the-top position still exists today. There may be fewer such positions, and you may have to sacrifice something in the process of getting there, but that position is still there.'

Louis elaborates on his point by using Absa's experience as an example of the kind of opportunities that are available. 'Barclays gave Absa the opportunity to work not only in South Africa but also in the rest of Africa, and today we can offer any person in Absa an international career.' So Louis says he would like to challenge that perception by suggesting that, if you feel restricted, you may be trapped in a certain stereotype. Given an international environment and all the opportunities of the continent, he believes that, if you are willing to move out of your comfort zone and to accept a degree of change, somewhere out there you will find the position that you want. But, as is the case with everything in today's world, you have to make it happen. Things aren't just going to happen by themselves and the opportunity is not going to drop into your lap; you have to go in search of it.

Louis moved around quite a bit in the course of his career and has been responsible for different regions of the country. What does he see as the value of these diverse responsibilities? You gain incredible experience and knowledge of human nature, he says. Louis reckons that you acquire experience 'by moving out of your comfort zone, by exploring new environments'. And, in the end, when you 'have to sit back and take difficult decisions, that experience you draw on is not something you just find in a manual; you gained it as a result of the road you have walked'. Many times you don't see the value of disruption while you are experiencing it, he adds, but you recognise it later, when you look back.

When it comes to banking, Louis declares that he is proud of the South African banking sector. He emphasises the value and necessity of a strong banking sector if you want to do business internationally, and also considers it important 'to say that we in South Africa want to have a leadership position on the African continent'. So you want a banking sector 'that is ranked among the better ones'; foreign as well as local investors want to be sure that they do business with institutions that safeguard their money.

The interview left me with a sense that Louis will continue to play a huge role in the development of young people and that he may focus on combining this with his love for sport. Perhaps Louis's career at Absa is not so much a case of someone who spent his entire working life with one employer, but rather a case of that employer never having been willing to let him go?

QUALITIES PEOPLE NEED TO GET TO THE TOP

- You must have the right technical knowledge and skills, 'combined with the book knowledge'.
- You must have the will to win. He believes that 'the will to win is a choice', and that it applies as much in the business world as in the world of sport. As a sport-mad businessman, Louis also conveyed this message to the Springbok team when he had the privilege of handing the players their jerseys before a Test against the All Blacks.
- Resoluteness, together with 'commitment to the vision and the strategy' of the business.

- The willingness to ensure that everything within an organisation 'is a balance between the hard, cold figures and the part that you play within a social environment to develop people and create opportunities for them'.
- You have to be able to form an opinion and to defend it. You must be able to think differently about things and should also be open to persuasion when faced with convincing facts and reasons.
- A strong personal value system, strong principles and an understanding of the Greater Plan.

CHAPTER 10

Dr Edwin Hertzog

FOUNDER AND EXECUTIVE CHAIRMAN OF THE MEDICLINIC INTERNATIONAL GROUP | *Interview broadcast on 6 September 2011*

Edwin qualified as an anaesthetist after 12 years of medical studies and spent three years in private practice. In January 1983 he joined the Rembrandt Group, of which his father Dirk was a co-founder and deputy chairman. After a concept presentation, Mediclinic was established later that year. The group listed on the JSE in 1986 and is today the sixth-largest private hospital group in the world, with hospitals in South Africa, Namibia, the Middle East and Switzerland. Edwin is currently executive chairman of the group and also serves on the boards of Remgro, Total (SA) and Distell, among others.

Edwin is an anaesthetist who practised privately for three years before exchanging his medical career for a position in the Rembrandt Group. Decisions of this nature are not taken lightly, and I started our conversation by asking him what prompted the change of direction. According to Edwin, Dr Anton Rupert invited him to join Rembrandt, on behalf of the board, as they had decided to involve the second generation of the original founder members in the company. Hence Edwin, together with Johann Rupert and one of his cousins, was invited to join the group with effect from January 1983. 'Whether I should have done this or not was, of course, a moot point,' he says. 'At the time I thought one should probably look at it in the same way as with a family farm, with the next generation having to decide whether they, too, want to be involved where the family assets are vested or otherwise leave the responsibility to professional managers.' In the end, he decided to try it out for three years and 'see how it goes'. For a medical doctor, the move was obviously 'a big jump'; in those days, Rembrandt was mainly a cigarette company that also had interests in the liquor industry. 'I had no idea as to what value I could add to the Rembrandt Group, but I took the plunge and got to work.' He thought he should perhaps first obtain an MBA or a formal business qualification, but Dr Rupert told him he had studied long enough: 'There are people here who can help you if necessary. There are books and magazines, carry on.'

It didn't take long for the medical background and the business world to find each other. Edwin began researching the viability of a new private hospital in the Western Cape. To put the idea into perspective, and perhaps to emphasise Edwin's vision, it is worth mentioning that, in the 1980s, some state hospitals offered among the best medical technology and services. Yet Edwin convinced the Rembrandt board to approve the proposed 120-bed Panorama Hospital in Cape Town's northern suburbs. Where did the idea of private healthcare originate? At the time when he was still a member of a private practice, Edwin explains, he had proposed to his nine partners that they develop their own day-surgery clinic with two theatres and a number of consulting rooms. He had investigated the possibility and presented a viability study to his partners, but 'eight of the nine rejected the idea out of hand'. With this background, he was asked in 1983 to do a presentation on the viability of a 120-bed hospital after a group of his specialist colleagues from the northern suburbs had approached the Rembrandt Group to consider an investment of this nature in view of the great need for more medical facilities in the area.

The plan was accepted and Rembrandt made the funds available. According to Edwin, this was where he got his lucky break. When he continued with his market research, there was so much support for a new hospital that they eventually opened Mediclinic Panorama with 325 beds instead of 120.

By 1986, the Mediclinic Group, then consisting of seven hospitals, was listed on the JSE. In 1987 global stock markets plummeted, however, and Mediclinic's share price was affected negatively. Moreover, the group failed to realise its profit forecasts. How did they experience this difficult period? Because the company had no profit history at the time of its listing, Edwin says, 'we had to do a five-year projection of our profit estimates. In the first three years we missed our estimates comfortably.' Every year he had to explain this underperformance to disappointed shareholders and try to cheer them up. Fortunately Mediclinic managed to make up for it in the fourth and fifth years, with the result that 'over the total five-year period, we beat our profit projections in total'.

As the group expanded, they built and acquired hospitals in various towns and cities across South Africa. But not in Edwin's home town of Stellenbosch; his father and Dr Rupert were opposed to the idea. So how did they eventually manage to establish the Mediclinic Stellenbosch? According to Edwin, his father and Dr Rupert had felt that the Stellenbosch community would be dead set against the development of a huge new building on account of the historic fabric of the town and 'the whole mindset of the residents'. Apart from the resistance they could expect from the community, they would also be letting themselves in for a lot of trouble 'because patients would come and complain to you'. But Edwin and his colleagues stuck to their guns: this was their work and they knew what they were doing. Many specialists were keen to practise in Stellenbosch and they were convinced that the town presented a good opportunity. They built the hospital in spite of the objections, 'and luckily it was a success story'.

The next giant leap came in 2007, with the takeover of the Hirslanden Group in Switzerland. This was a quantum shift that doubled the size of the Mediclinic Group. But the decision behind the acquisition had a strategic run-up and fitted into a longer-term strategy. As Edwin explains it, they had realised in 2005 that it was no longer really possible for the group to expand on a large scale in South Africa. Firstly, the local market was too small and, secondly, the Competition Commission had begun to impose certain limits that restricted expansion. 'Therefore we started thinking that perhaps we should diversify geographically. One thing we always knew was that we liked our business very much, and we didn't want to diversify seriously beyond our core business.'

Thus they began to look for opportunities in other countries. When specialists who worked in Mediclinic hospitals in the Western Cape suggested that they consider Dubai, 'we went there with them and got a foot in the door'. According to Edwin, their business in Dubai, where they currently operate two hospitals and eight clinics, was 'not a very big enterprise', but it gave them 'a bit of confidence, a bit of exposure to the outside world'. So when the Hirslanden opportunity cropped up in 2007, they were ready to grasp it. Edwin explains that Hirslanden is by far the largest private hospital group in Switzerland, with almost 40% of that country's private hospital beds.

To progress from a plan for a single 120-bed hospital to more than 9 000 beds in four countries, with 4 000 medical specialists involved in the group, is a massive achievement. I asked Edwin whether they have achieved what they initially envisaged with the establishment of Mediclinic. They have always believed that they must be good at what they do, he says. 'We must be profitable, and we must add value for our shareholders as well as for the communities where we operate hospitals.' In his opinion, he adds, a better measure by which to judge a company is its number of employees, 'because that shows for how many people and their dependants you, as an employer, are responsible. At present we have just over 23 000 employees.'

In his speeches, Edwin often emphasises what they at Mediclinic call 'the science of care'. This is something that is close to his heart, he says. 'The evolution of medical science shows us that service delivery by doctors worldwide has advanced because of scientific progress. In other words, new techniques, new equipment and new medicines that have been developed are based on scientific research that has been statistically proven. Unfortunately, there are many service and product providers out there that lead people up the garden path and, in fact, exploit them.' In the Mediclinic Group they have told themselves that they should also strive to put the care of patients, 'the nursing care and the other friendly help that one would expect in hospitals', on a 'scientific platform'.

The global debate about the most cost-effective provision of healthcare is likely to continue for decades to come. I was interested in hearing Edwin's views on the proposed South African National Health Insurance scheme. The health insurance system is a financial system, he says, while the problem with our current system in the public sector is poor service delivery. Improved service delivery requires good facilities and equipment, sufficient numbers of the right personnel and good management. 'One can pump more money into the system, but this isn't necessarily going to produce better service delivery.' What he is very pleased about, however, is that the system is going to be phased in over a long enough period and that pilot projects will be undertaken. Edwin reckons that many lessons will be learnt and adjustments made in the coming years.

At heart, Edwin is still a doctor with an inherent sense of responsibility towards people. How does he view the leadership role of medical doctors in society? He believes that medical training inculcates 'that discipline of scientific thinking and service to your fellow human beings', and that, for this reason, people tend to regard doctors as role models and leaders. 'A society is driven by its role models, and medical doctors are generally aware of their responsibility in this regard – I have no doubt about that.' They do have a problem in that they often don't have enough time to devote to the obligations of leadership positions, 'but many of them are prepared to take up such roles in society and to make time for it'. In his own case, he has been involved in school governing bodies, and served as a member of the council of Stellenbosch University for ten years, including a stint as chairman. He describes his term on the council as a very enriching experience, 'and I'm glad I did it'.

I had wondered at first about the interface between an anaesthetist and a business giant like the Rembrandt Group of 1982. The absolute focus on the human being and quality healthcare is where the two came together in Mediclinic. I find it hard to imagine that anyone except a dyed-in-the-wool medical practitioner would have been able to build up this group to what is today. Despite Edwin being a highly successful entrepreneur and businessman, I do believe that the medical focus on caring about one's fellow human beings has played a greater role in what he has achieved with Mediclinic. Dr Rupert was right; Edwin did not need an MBA to help him reach great heights.

Edwin describes his leadership style as 'situational leadership'. Leaders must be able to position themselves according to the specific situation they are faced with. 'In the 28 years at Mediclinic there have been different cycles, different seasons. I believe that your leadership style must be adaptable to those circumstances in which you find yourself. I like to compare it to a golfer. I'm an avid golfer myself – you have a set of clubs in your bag, and, hole for hole, you need to decide which club will serve you best in order to get the best score at this particular hole.'

WHY HE RECOMMENDS THE MEDICAL FIELD AS A CAREER CHOICE

- Medicine is an interesting and rapidly developing environment that is at the cutting edge of technology.
- Medicine is a very wide world with different specialist fields and an enormous number of opportunities, not only if you are a specialist, but also as a general practitioner or medical official.
- You are able to find work in 'virtually any town in any country of the world'.
- It's a satisfying career that adds value – not only for yourself and your family, but also for the community.

CHAPTER 11

Nick Vlok

FOUNDER AND EXECUTIVE CHAIRMAN OF DIGICORE
Interview broadcast on 13 September 2011

Nick obtained a BCom degree at the former Rand Afrikaans University (University of Johannesburg), majoring in Transport Economics. In 1985 he started his own fleet management business with R2 000 in capital. DigiCore was listed on the JSE in 1998. Today this fleet management and vehicle tracking technology group operates on six continents and employs more than 1 000 people. After a period as non-executive chairman, Nick has returned to an executive position, still as chairman.

DigiCore is one of those entrepreneurial stories of someone who built a business and then listed it just before the market experienced a decline. What differentiates DigiCore from most of the technology companies of the late 1990s, however, is that the company is still here today and can boast of a market value of several hundreds of millions of rands.

In 1985, a young Nick started his own fleet management company with just R2 000 in initial capital. He is proud of the fact that, in spite of the company's small size, they managed to pay all their accounts and salaries every month from the outset. Many new businesses collapse in the first six to 12 months, and I wanted to find out from Nick what they focused on in those first years. What helped a lot, he says, is that he had been involved in the fleet management industry before 1985. Thus he had a client base he could approach, and he also had relationships with suppliers, which allowed him to buy on credit. That was important, because 'with R2 000 you can't really start a business, as you know'. He recalls how hard they worked – '18 hours a day, really seven days a week'. Their prices were fair and their service 'absolutely exceptional'. One of the things they did differently in terms of service was to go out to clients' premises instead of clients having to bring their vehicles to workshops.

From 1985 to 1996 the business was built up, with the emphasis on growth. The point of departure was that external capital was not really available; they had to use their own capital. How did they manage to grow sustainably over ten years? According to Nick, they stuck to 'the recipe' they had followed at the beginning and mostly grew organically. With takeovers, they 'looked very carefully at the risks and, of course, the benefits' of a transaction, took a decision, and then usually 'went back to the bank and obtained financing'. When your house is at stake, he adds, 'it forces you to work a little bit harder and to think more carefully. The fact that we had to capitalise it ourselves also played a role in the growth, but, all the same, we took risks at times and then just put in the work.'

The late 1990s saw the start of a new phase for the business. Many companies grow for a number of years but then arrive at a crossroads, where a choice has to be made about the road ahead. There are usually two alternatives: you either grow at the same rate or you decide to take a huge leap. DigiCore opted for the latter, and the decision resulted in the listing of the group on the JSE in December 1998. When I ask why they decided on the listing route, Nick explains that he had realised that his company, which was then still known as Vepro, needed a national network, as well as new technology that had become available. But to implement their plans, they needed cash. To a lesser degree, he says, the listing was maybe aimed at 'unlocking a bit of value for some of the shareholders, but it was primarily in order to grow and to consolidate the required technology and the existing factory'.

After the successful listing, the technology bubble burst in the United States, with the result that the rug was pulled out from under technology shares. DigiCore's shares fell to 17c at a point, and it was rumoured that South African technology companies were doomed. Most of the newly listed local technology companies bit the dust, yet DigiCore survived. What distinguished them from the many others that failed? Nick reckons 'it was a matter of continuing to invest in technology. We were conscious of the fact that we constantly had to stay ahead in our specific industry.' He admits that the company was going through a tough time by 2000 – 'our cash flow wasn't very good at that stage'. According to Nick, they had 'a bit of luck' that year when they secured a deal with Debis, which had taken over the management of Telkom's fleet of about 20 000 vehicles. 'It gave us that boost we could use in the following ten years to really sustain the growth.'

It is interesting that successful entrepreneurs often talk about luck. On closer scrutiny, however, one generally finds that it was a matter of the right products with the right service at the right price, together with perseverance, and then the stroke of luck – that 'luck' was made and earned!

I wanted us to focus a bit more on the listing, the challenges that accompanied it, and why DigiCore managed to recover while other companies folded. When he casts his mind back to the listing, Nick says: 'It was of course fantastic because we suddenly had a lot of cash at our disposal, so things went swimmingly for the first year or two.' On the other hand, it also brought problems; for example, as a result of the companies that had bought into DigiCore, Nick suddenly had 14 directors and each one had his own approach. Once the cash ran dry, the shock 'brought us back to earth a bit' and made them focus on the philosophy of 'looking after the pennies so that the pounds will look after themselves'. According to Nick, this was a principle that drove them throughout, 'that you really need to be careful with your funds and that cash is very important'. What made DigiCore successful, he reckons, is that the company kept to the recipe it still has today: loyal people, hard work, good service, and constantly striving to develop new products and being first to market.

In response to my question about the highlights of the past years, Nick first singles out the listing. And when their market capitalisation exceeded R2 billion, in 2008, 'it was most definitely a highlight'. In elaborating on some of their success stories, he stresses the fact that it is 'absolutely South African technology' with which they outcompeted global players to win tenders in Britain from companies such as Thames Water, Royal Mail and Network Rail. As far as local transactions are concerned, he considers the deal with the South African Police Service a milestone. Even the transaction with BHP Billiton in Australia, 'which proved to be quite a challenge, but one that we overcame', he includes among their milestones.

As we talk about their business, the better times as well as the tough periods, Nick constantly emphasises the importance of 'sticking to the recipe and doing business ethically'. DigiCore has had its share of obstacles and difficulties; yet each time Nick and his team have managed to surmount the challenges. Their recipe has served them well over the years.

ADVICE TO YOUNG ENTREPRENEURS

- Make sure that you get an educational qualification. 'I would suggest a BCom or something of that nature; it has proved vital to me over the years to have the financial background, even in a technology company.'
- Choose an industry that you like. 'My sense is that you should then preferably work in that industry for about three years until you really feel sure that you are ready to start your own enterprise.'
- You must have a competitive advantage. 'You must at least know how you are going to stand out above the other guys in the field; otherwise you won't make it.'
- You must be prepared to 'put in the hours' and hang in there for the first few years, wasting no money but instead building up a cash buffer for when the hard times hit you, 'because those times will come'.
- Always do business on an ethical basis, no matter how tough things may be.

CHAPTER 12

Whitey Basson

CHIEF EXECUTIVE OF THE SHOPRITE GROUP

Interview broadcast on 20 September 2011

Whitey grew up in Porterville in the Western Cape. He studied at Stellenbosch University, qualified as a chartered accountant, and joined the Pep Stores Group in 1971. In 1979 Pep bought a chain of eight Shoprite stores in the Western Cape. Today Whitey is the chief executive of a group comprising more than 1300 corporate stores and 460 franchise outlets in 17 countries.

If there is one company that can pride itself on doing business successfully in countries across Africa, it is undoubtedly the retail giant Shoprite, with its Shoprite and Checkers stores, led by Whitey Basson. Today this achievement is almost taken for granted in a field where many other companies have taken a beating.

Having started his career as a chartered accountant, how did Whitey end up in the retail sector? When I ask him about his move to the Pep Stores Group in 1971, Whitey explains that he never really planned to become an accountant. He had even considered medicine, probably because the doctor in his home town of Porterville 'drove the best-looking cars'. Eventually he opted for a BCom degree and qualified as a chartered accountant (CA). At an accounting firm where he worked, he especially enjoyed visiting the retail companies they had as clients. Another reason he was drawn to retail was the fact that his father, a farmer, also owned liquor stores. 'So, as a child I grew up with buying and selling.' In short, he says, he 'happened to know something about retail' and 'liked his retail clients a lot'.

Shoprite started from humble beginnings in 1979 with the purchase by Pep of a small chain of eight stores in the Western Cape. The group currently consists of more than 1 300 corporate stores and 460 franchise outlets in 17 countries, and has a turnover in excess of R85 billion. Did he ever think in those early days that this was where they were headed? 'Yes, I didn't only think so,' he replies immediately. At that stage the Pep Stores Group had taken a decision to explore the potential of food retailing and had looked at various models, such as overseas partners. 'Our models were always based on growing very big, very quickly.'

In the business world, one often sees companies that begin to grow but never really get out of the starting blocks; they reach a certain level and then stagnate. When I ask Whitey how they approached the challenge of building an eight-store group into a 'serious player', he says that 'playing' was exactly what it was. 'We enjoyed it. It was, like, a few young guys who ventured forth – mostly with good retail knowledge and other disciplines they could apply – and we really just played against our biggest opposition at that stage in the Western Cape; we played bush war, cat and mouse.' It was an exciting time, he says, with the highlights coming from the fact that you were starting with something small and pitting yourself against the mighty Goliath. Each time you won something, you got 'that incredible adrenaline injection that told you, let's go for the next step'.

A huge jump in the growth of the business came in 1997, when they bought OK Bazaars from the then SA Breweries for just R1 in a much-discussed deal. The R1 purchase of a group of 150 stores caused a sensation, but most people failed to take into account that OK Bazaars was losing about R1 million a day at that stage, with 33 000 jobs at stake. How did they manage to stem the losses and turn these stores around?

According to Whitey, at least he had the benefit of the experience gained through other acquisitions, in which the Pep Stores Group had turned businesses around and integrated them. Besides Half Price Stores, a number of Ackermans stores and Grand Bazaars, 'Checkers was of course a big lesson for us, because in the case of both Checkers and OK their losses almost exceeded our profits'. Because of what they had learnt from the acquisition and incorporation of Checkers, OK was not 'a terribly dramatic takeover'.

People always talk of the R1, he remarks, 'but that was just the stamp that was on the contract; it was actually an entirely different transaction'. Although they were ready to take over OK, it was still 'nerve-wracking, because if you're losing that kind of money per day you have to work very swiftly and very hard. But it wasn't that we were scared of doing it or that we didn't believe we were capable of turning it around.'

One of Shoprite's major achievements is their success in Africa, where they operate in 16 countries besides South Africa. What does Whitey regard as their recipe for doing business in Africa? Why has

Shoprite managed to overcome the hurdles that have tripped up other companies, and, on the face of it, to do so with ease? Whitey begins his answer in his typical tongue-in-cheek way with 'I don't know' before continuing in a more serious vein: 'You need to look at it against the backdrop of us having a culture of building things up from scratch, changing and working with them and overcoming problems. We didn't inherit a business that had a clean system with good computers and pretty desks. We are used to working together as a team to change things, and Africa has the kind of problems smaller businesses would also have. Africa is actually full of small businesses and perhaps we have just found easier methods of overcoming problems – not that we've overcome all of them. There are still thousands of problems you sit with every day, and they usually have to do with red tape.'

In his view, what differentiated them from other retail players that had ventured into Africa was that they were 'fairly expert' by that time. 'If you opened a store in Kuruman while living in the Cape, you've already learnt to cross the rivers.' In summary, he says, it was easier for them thanks to 'that kind of game pattern and also people who have already done it bit by bit'.

When I ask him how he succeeds in managing Shoprite's 1 300 corporate stores from his office in the Western Cape, Whitey says straight out: 'I don't.' But he is quick to explain that his statement is not as dramatic as it sounds. At Shoprite, they 'have a very strong discipline structure within the business'. No one encroaches on another person's terrain, but they retain 'that one crucial aspect that people shouldn't lose their entrepreneurial skills'. It is not really a case of him managing 1 300 shops and 95 000 employees. There are different regions that he visits monthly or more frequently; these are all managed independently, with their own managing directors, financial directors and other staff. 'So when you eventually have your structure in place, you are managing a lot of small businesses that are combined into these 95 000 people.'

Whitey loves to drop in on Shoprite and Checkers stores, especially when he is on holiday. 'I have this bad habit that it's my passion to look at stores,' he admits, 'and it's my passion to make sure that my stores are in order.' If he doesn't drop in on the stores, 'there are usually people dropping in on me to tell me what's wrong'. According to Whitey, one of his colleagues remarked that he has 'a kind of management style of walking in at the back door', and the most characteristic feature is that 'it's a management style of chaos'.

When I read through some of the Shoprite annual reports in preparation for the interview, I was struck by the recurring theme of improving people's circumstances and the fact that Shoprite creates between 5000 and 7000 new jobs every year. How do they give expression to this goal of improving circumstances in practice? Whitey says that 'from day one it has been the policy of our group, and also something that has been very close to my heart, to change people and to be able to give them better opportunities'. They give their employees' children 'first options, if they are sufficiently qualified to do the work', and 'make sure that all people within the group are evaluated and that they can move to better positions'.

There are thousands of people in the group 'who started at the bottom of the business as shelf packers and now occupy high positions'. For Whitey, the 'nicest thing' is that some of their children are doctors and professors today, 'and you know that you've been part of the process' of helping people to grow and giving them opportunities. He values the fact that 'it gives you that loyalty of the people who work with you, plus that satisfaction when you walk past someone one day and he says, "Meet my wife and my son, who has just completed his studies." That gives me a wonderful feeling.'

When we touch on the value of hard work, Whitey comments that this does not mean you should 'work hard stupidly'. But he believes that you should work hard every day of your life and that a problem should be disposed of quickly. Not settling a problem immediately is like 'scoring a try on the 25-yard line'. 'We conclude the transaction over the telephone and then confirm in a proper way what the transaction was, but there aren't any loose ends that you drag along with you. So there's nothing of this terribly academic style of thinking which then leads to a nil result.' What it comes down to for him, is 'tackling a problem, solving it, finalising it and putting it away'.

I concluded the interview with a question about the honorary doctorate Whitey was awarded by Stellenbosch University in 2010. What did this recognition mean to him? A deeply emotional gratitude was visible in his eyes as he replied to my question, and his voice couldn't hide the fact that this formidable international businessman considered it a momentous accolade. To him, it was 'just incredibly nice to know that an ordinary bloke like me who came from a small rural town, worked hard, did reasonably well at university, could reach a point where people like the professors and university management said that this bloke is good enough to represent our university too and to receive an honorary doctorate from it'.

When he recounts how he went home after the graduation ceremony and thought 'my dad would have been proud of me', you realise that the aim of improving people's lives will remain a reality in Whitey's Shoprite Group.

WHY HE RECOMMENDS RETAILING AS A CAREER CHOICE

- It's a good business to be in from a financial perspective. 'People make very good money.'
- It's enjoyable work, with 'a wide sphere of different facets in which you can operate – from property to computer science to buying'.
- You are free to 'go and do things and to create'.
- It's not just a white-collar career, because 'one moment you're carrying a box and the next moment you have to finalise a big contract'.

CHAPTER 13

Dr Johan van Zyl

CHIEF EXECUTIVE OF SANLAM
Interview broadcast on 18 January 2012

Johan, who grew up on a farm, holds two doctorates, one in Agricultural Economics from the University of Pretoria (UP) and one in Economics from Vista University. In his academic career, he was dean of the Agricultural Sciences faculty and later rector of UP, as well as a professor at Michigan State University in the USA. His international experience also includes a stint at the World Bank as coordinator of rural development. In 2001 Johan entered the private sector, first being appointed chief executive of Santam and subsequently chief executive of Sanlam, the position he still holds today. Since Johan took over as CEO of Sanlam in 2003, the group's market value has increased fivefold and Sanlam is once again recognised as a market leader in its field.

Before talking to Johan about Sanlam and the group's growth since his appointment as chief executive in 2003, I wanted to touch on two other elements in his career: agriculture and academia.

I started by asking him about his views on South African farmers. Johan reckons that, over the years, 'they have built up an incredible industry that was actually the pioneer of economic growth in South Africa'. This has been achieved in spite of the particular challenges farmers face in this country. He emphasises specifically the environment within which farmers have to operate: the climate is not the easiest, or the most suitable, for farming; there are problems with infrastructure; and we are far removed from international markets. Would he nonetheless recommend farming to young people as a career? 'Any time,' he says unreservedly. Food is an essential commodity and 'it is increasingly becoming more expensive, because the world population is growing and food is getting scarcer. So, the opportunities are there.'

Johan was a successful academic, both locally and in the United States, who ended up occupying the position of rector at the University of Pretoria. What motivated his decision to exchange academia for the business world? He explains that he became rector of the university at a relatively young age, but, in his view, it is rather a job for someone nearing the end of his or her career. 'Spending year after year in an environment of a repetitive nature isn't really what I wanted to do in my life. I was rector for five years – I think that's enough, and that one should then step aside and make way for others.'

Did he find that there were differences between the South African and the American students he taught? In certain respects, Johan says, students everywhere are basically the same; they want to have fun, do as little as possible and get as much as possible. But, in his opinion, South African students are in a unique position. 'While other people learn about things that are remote and take place elsewhere in the world, many of those things are happening right here on our doorstep: for instance, transformation, economic change, political change.' He believes that our students 'really have an inside track', and holds the view that the success South Africans tend to achieve internationally can be attributed to their 'much wider field of experience'. 'Many of the things other people have to learn about are almost innate in us. I think it's truly a privilege to be a South African.'

According to Johan's CV, he assumed his position at Sanlam on 31 March 2003. Why such an unusual date? He acknowledges with a smile that he was actually supposed to start on 1 April but wanted to avoid being an April fool, 'since you never how the future is going to turn out. So I thought it safer to start on the 31st.'

The Sanlam of 2003 was a far cry from the market leader of today. For one thing, the company's share price in 2011 was five times higher than it had been when he took over the reins. I wanted to find out from Johan how he approached the task of getting the company back into shape. Initially, he says, you just have to play the hand you have been dealt. Everyone likes to have only the best cards, but life doesn't work that way. 'You must do what is possible and start with small steps before you begin to walk and eventually to start jogging a bit.' Sanlam did have a clear path and idea of where they wanted to go, and as they managed to get some of the things right, 'the possibilities ahead increased'. Johan stresses the fact that the turnaround was not a solo effort. 'Managing a business is about a team of people. It's a much greater effort. It's about many people who all make contributions, and it's actually a privilege to be able to succeed in cooperation with others.'

He clearly puts a great emphasis on people, and accordingly made a number of big appointments in those first few years in order to strengthen the team. Johan uses the example of a tangible product such as a car to illustrate the importance of having the right people in the financial services industry. 'You can sit in a car, you can inhale that new-car smell, and you know you're going to buy that car. We, on the other hand, have nothing to show you – what does our product look like? You're only as good as the person sitting across the table who makes the promise that we're going to look after you, mostly that we will pay out to your family after your death. Our industry is about promises, and there you need good people. You can't achieve success in financial services without the best people.'

How does one approach the responsibility of looking after the wealth of so many South Africans? The first thing, Johan remarks, 'is to treat the money as if it's your own and not to take chances. I think if one also looks at Sanlam, we don't try to take big risks or get rich quickly, whether for ourselves or for clients.' They attempt to limit the risks that people take; if they do take risks, the risk must 'relate to the possibilities and the returns that are available, but also to the appetite of the people whose money we're dealing with. I think that is probably the crucial thing.'

Sanlam is a big ship, with many employees and numerous specialists in various departments. How would he describe his own management style? In terms of the academic literature, 'I would say a somewhat eclectic order, but in ordinary language it really just means a bit of everything', Johan says. 'You have to stay in control of things, but you need to give people opportunities and it has to be about a team.' His background is in agriculture and he isn't an actuary, which means that he won't know everything. You must be able to rely on people who are experts in their field, and you have to surround yourself with the right people. Johan singles out negativity as a mindset to avoid. 'You need to have people with a positive outlook, people who want to do something.' They are the ones you should take along with you and to whom you should give opportunities.

Johan has worked outside South Africa on two occasions; would he recommend to others an opportunity to gain international experience? What was personally of value to him, he says, was discovering that the things with which we battle every day in South Africa are actually the same problems everyone else in the world is grappling with. 'We're not as unique as we like to think. There are many things that are enjoyable in our country, and so on, but as a result of such exposure you look more widely at the world and you also measure yourself a bit against what is happening elsewhere.'

I asked Johan about the qualities he looks for in people when identifying leadership and potential. What distinguishes successful people from the rest of the field? It goes without saying that they need to have certain attributes, such as reliability and punctuality, he says. But when you look more closely at those who are going to excel, the ones who 'bring you something above the ordinary', there are few of them. 'You look for people who constantly have new ideas. The entrepreneurs. Even in big organisations that are often bureaucratic, the entrepreneurs are the people who give you the ideas, and then you have to create the opportunity for them. That something extra. The extra mile you are prepared to go. That's what it's really about.'

After the interview was broadcast, I received a call from Johan's extremely efficient personal assistant, Almarie Fourie, requesting a copy for the Sanlam community: 'The employees are proud of their boss!' I reckon there are few people who can boast of having been at the helm of one of the country's biggest universities as well as one of its most successful financial services groups within the space of a decade. Sanlam's employees and clients have good reason to be proud of their chief executive.

ADVICE TO YOUNG PEOPLE

- You must set goals for yourself, and aim high. 'You often surprise yourself by finding that very high goals can be reached.'
- You must have a plan. 'Things don't happen by chance, and, if you don't have a plan, you end up in places where you don't want to be.'
- You must work hard, which means that 'you need to work a bit harder than the next guy' to become really successful.

INVESTMENT PRINCIPLES

- Most people who retire don't have enough money, not because they made the wrong investments, but because they started saving too late in life.
- Don't stop working too soon. Retiring at 60 'is a historical thing, dating from the time when people died at a younger age'. Instead of simply retiring, get yourself another occupation, do other things – there are many opportunities available in this regard.
- Don't invest money where you think you are going to get rich quickly; you shouldn't gamble with your retirement money.
- Look at the risk and balance of your investment portfolio so that you don't lose your retirement money if something small goes wrong.
- Get an expert adviser and, remember, 'if he promises too much, he's not a good adviser'.

CHAPTER 14

Andries van Heerden

CHIEF EXECUTIVE OF AFRIMAT
Interview broadcast on 25 January 2012

Andries qualified as a mechanical engineer at the former Potchefstroom University and later obtained an MBA degree at the University of Stellenbosch Business School. He started his career at Iscor Mining and, after a stint in the packaging industry, joined Prima Quarries in 2001. This first venture into the open-pit mining industry eventually led to Afrimat, a JSE-listed supplier of construction materials and industrial minerals.

Each interview had a distinctive element that stood out when I reflected on it afterwards. In Andries's case, it was the role of mentors; he identified role models who contributed from time to time, and at crucial periods in his life, to his personal success. Our conversation reminded me of the fact that all of us have benefited from role models and mentors in our careers. Perhaps many people deny this, either deliberately or unwittingly, or simply don't notice the part such figures have played. Or maybe it is about an attitude of allowing others to play a positive role in one's development? Be that as it may, Andries emphasises and acknowledges the role of mentors in his achievements.

His appreciation of the inspiring role of mentors started during Andries's formative years as a mechanical engineering student. He stresses the example set by his elder brother who, at a relatively young age, was not only a professor but 'also renowned in the world for his expertise as an econometrician'. It demonstrated to him at the time 'what one can achieve by working hard and in a disciplined way, and by being willing to make some sacrifices and put pressure on oneself'.

After completing his studies, Andries started working as an engineer at Iscor Mining. His first boss was another mentor, Matie von Wielligh, who would later play a huge role in his business and also become chairman of Afrimat. Andries considers himself 'extremely privileged' to have worked under the 'outstanding' management team at Ellisras, 'one of Iscor Mining's flagship mines at the time'. He has high praise for what he learnt from Matie as a leader. Matie was very interested in them as young engineers 'and also really believed in me'. According to Andries, 'he often pushed me to do things I myself didn't believe I could achieve, which was incredibly important for a young guy's self-image and his ability to practise his profession'.

Later in the 1990s he left the mining industry for a job at a packaging company and also acquired an MBA in 2000. The motivation behind these moves, explains Andries, is that his dream was 'to go into business eventually, to become an entrepreneur'. At Iscor he had advanced as an engineer and was increasingly given greater responsibilities, 'but I learnt very little about the other aspects of a business'. Besides financial and human resource management, he felt the need to learn more about marketing, which was not so important in the case of a commodities company. The benefit of the shift to the packaging company was that he 'got very good exposure to the entire spectrum of business'.

In 2001 Andries joined Prima Quarries, an open-pit mining company, where he later became managing director. But here the pursuit of his dream would lead to the loss of his job. As Andries explains it, in 2003 Prima concluded the first black empowerment deal in the quarrying industry. 'We saw opportunities at the time and that there was a role for a national player, which made me very excited. But the process implied that we had to list on the JSE.' This was not exactly what Prima's shareholders had in mind, with the result that they and Andries parted ways – 'which was very, very bad for me'. Andries describes the experience as a low point in his life and a massive shock. 'One day I was the managing director of a company who saw myself as successful and who received good feedback, and literally the next day I was unemployed.'

He emphasises, however, that he learnt a great deal from this setback – 'the importance of having a good home to return to' and being able to count on the positive support of his wife, and 'the importance of picking oneself up'. As he puts it: 'It's no use staying down if the horse has thrown you. You have to get back into the saddle as soon as possible and get going again, and that's what we tried to do at the time.'

When the 40-year-old Andries unexpectedly found himself jobless, there was once again a mentor who played a major part in getting him back onto the horse. Laurie Korsten was the person who immediately started advising him, helped him to overcome his despondency, and became actively involved with him in a new plan to bring Andries's dream to fruition. Laurie assisted him in the acquisition of the Lancaster Group, which merged with Prima to form a new company,

Afrimat. According to Andries, Laurie 'was not only the egg in the breakfast, he was literally the bacon in the breakfast in helping me make a success of this'.

Following a number of acquisitions, Afrimat is today a JSE-listed company with a turnover in excess of R1 billion, 1 600 employees and a market value of R650 million. Was this Andries's dream? Partly, he says: 'We are on the way.' He quotes Apple co-founder Steve Jobs: 'If you're not busy being born, you're busy dying.' As Andries sees it, 'We're still being born, we're still growing, but this is all part of the dream and it's exciting to see this dream unfolding.'

Andries lays great emphasis on the principle of having a dream that you pursue, but also says that many people throw in their hand just before they realise their dream. When I ask him to elaborate, he explains that you will always run into obstacles when following a dream. Maybe a law changes, or you fail to obtain financing on your first attempt, and so you give up and use this blow as an excuse. He feels very strongly that you should not throw in the towel too soon. 'If you know that something will work and you know how it's going to work, drive it, persevere, don't give up.' But you should also be realistic: 'It's no use trying to flog a dead donkey back to life.' If your plan is not feasible, you should 'face the brutal facts', as Jim Collins says, and realise that you need to abandon it. What it boils down to, in Andries's view, is that you should exercise good judgement.

The construction industry and related industries went through deep waters in 2009 as a result of the recession, which severely dented confidence. As chief executive of a business that stood at the centre of this and managed to pull through successfully, how did he deal with the challenges? Andries believes that, in such a difficult time, when everyone is fearful and nervous about their own future and that of the business, it is crucial for a leader 'to hold his head high and show people that there is hope'. The body language of the leader, the person who sees the whole picture, is to many people outside the company a sign either that the game is up or that there is hope; if you can succeed in getting that right, you've already achieved a lot. Secondly, a leader should also be realistic and have a good understanding of the right path on which to lead his people out of this tough situation. According to Andries, this means that you should really listen to your people, garner as much advice as possible from outside, and also exercise good judgement in respect of what you choose to listen to or to ignore. 'Then you have to be able to indicate a path, and people should be able to trust that you will lead them out of the present difficulties.'

We concluded our conversation by touching on what the building of infrastructure can contribute towards putting South Africa on a winning trajectory. Andries reckons that we can learn a lesson from the hosting of the Fifa World Cup in 2010. What stands out for him is that everyone shared the common goal of a successful tournament and was excited about it. There was structure, purposeful action, discipline and order. 'We all focused on the same thing.' Our main challenge in South Africa, he believes, is to achieve 'that common focus' and to 'get ourselves oriented and disciplined so that the entire country gets behind that common goal'. What should follow from this is that 'we then meticulously and methodically implement what is required and progress towards a better dispensation, particularly in economic terms, and that we can get the economy going so that we create jobs and overcome the challenges facing us'.

MANAGEMENT PHILOSOPHY

Andries's management philosophy rests on two pillars: empowering competent people, and doing the right things in the right way:
- You can't play in the A league with B-team and C-team players. You must have competent and capable people who can do their work well without you having to look after them, but then you must

empower them. 'It's no use getting the best players on the team and then restricting them and not allowing them to do their job properly. You need to have that good balance where you empower people, but within a culture of discipline and structure.'

- You have to know what the right things are that should be done in every situation. 'What should you focus on? Which things add value and which are merely time consumers?' Doing something 'the right way' refers to quality, 'a certain ethos of attention to detail in order to ensure that things are finalised correctly and completely so that they lead to results and are not half-baked'.

KEY POINTS FOR SUCCESS

- **Know yourself** – 'The good Lord gave each of us specific gifts and talents – keep to yours and build on them. Make sure that you stay within your particular area of strengths.'
- **Self-discipline** – 'Make sure that you plan your life and that your life is disciplined.'
- **Acquire mentors and learn from others** – 'None of us has all the answers, and the more people you can learn from, the better your chances of getting a good end result.'

CHAPTER 15

Hubert Brody

CHIEF EXECUTIVE OF THE IMPERIAL GROUP

Interview broadcast on 1 February 2012

Hubert's father was a medical doctor. His decision to study accountancy was almost accidental; as someone said to him, 'If you don't really know what to study, become a CA.' His studies at Stellenbosch University were followed by 13 years in the banking sector, with the last three at Imperial Bank in the Imperial Group. In 2007 Hubert was appointed unexpectedly as CEO of the group. He took over the reins as the global financial crisis hit, and many observers expected him to flounder on account of his relative youth and lack of experience. But Hubert surprised the market; today Imperial is still one of South Africa's most successful groups, boasting a market value of more than R40 billion. Under his leadership, Imperial has also made some of its biggest international acquisitions.

knew from my earlier interaction with Hubert that he is usually very serious and that interviews would not exactly come naturally to him. Over the years, however, I have seen how his confidence in dealing with the media has grown – perhaps partly because he has such a remarkable story to tell. From being an unknown accountant in an industrial group to becoming one of South Africa's top business leaders in less than decade!

I started our conversation with his 13 years in the banking sector. What did banking experience contribute to his success? Hubert describes it as a 'very good training school' and singles out two aspects that proved to be important for him. One was his exposure to balance-sheet management and to managing the bank's financing. Later, at Imperial, he says, 'it was fairly critical to handle this correctly'. Secondly, he benefited from the experience of granting credit and loans to businesses, which gave him 'a good sense of how successful businesses develop and what to look for in order to spot potential in a business'.

No conversation with the CEO of Imperial would be complete without a mention of the group's legendary founder. In 1971, 27-year-old Irishman Bill Lynch arrived in South Africa poor and jobless, and over time transformed a single failing car dealership into one of the country's leading industrial groups, with 40 000 employees and a market value of R30 billion. In 2006 Lynch became the first South African to win the Ernst & Young World Entrepreneur of the Year award. I wanted to take Hubert back to 2000, the year he joined the group, and get his impressions of Imperial in those days under Lynch.

According to Hubert, the company 'started small – new ideas were constantly added and tried out, and, in cases where they worked, they grew into something very, very big'. The start of the car rental business, he says, 'is an incredibly beautiful story'; the company had extra vehicles and so asked themselves, 'What can we do with these vehicles?' The truck and van rental business arose out of this. Hubert refers to the history of Imperial Bank as an equally beautiful story. Bill and the team, he explains, were of the view that other people were making too much money from Imperial as far as motor vehicle financing was concerned. 'We did all the hard work of selling the cars, but there was a lot of valuable annuity income that Imperial felt was due to us.' Hubert says that 'Bill looked at this opportunity and said eventually, let's close our eyes a bit, get ourselves a banking licence, and off we go.' It was, of course, much more complex than they had ever imagined, he adds.

In 2000, Imperial Bank had assets of R1.5 billion, which meant it was actually 'a tiny bank'. Bill then told the management team that the bank would reach assets of R50 billion in ten years' time. 'We just took this with a pinch of salt, because how on Earth would it be possible?' But Bill 'motivated people and created that bigger picture'. In 2010 they sold Imperial Bank to Nedbank as a very successful organisation, with assets to the value of R55 million.

Bill Lynch died early in 2008 after a long illness, but in 2007 the board had decided to appoint a young ('inexperienced' was the media's preferred term) Hubert Brody to succeed him as chief executive. Was Hubert, like the rest of South Africa's business sector, surprised by the appointment?

'Nothing quite prepares you for such a position,' he admits, 'and at the beginning it is fairly tough because there are so many new things.' He stresses the importance of the team you have around you in such circumstances; you need to be sure that it's a team that can reach great heights. Specifically at that time, he needed to be sure that it could get the group through a very difficult period. 'I really had confidence in the fact that we had an extremely strong team – people with profound experience in their respective industries – and believed that if one were to direct the team correctly and implement some of the structural changes we had to make, we actually had a great future ahead of us. I was always very positive about that.'

Hubert couldn't have chosen a worse time to take over the reins: the global financial crisis hit, economies were plunged into recession, and the value of Imperial shares halved. On top of that, Imperial had debts of about R20 billion, with banks tightening their purse strings. For the new CEO, this state of affairs gave fresh meaning to the expression 'thrown in at the deep end'. My question to him was simple: how does one deal with such a situation?

In the first place, it was vital to have a plan, Hubert says. As a management team, they had already talked a lot about what that plan should be. Hence they had a strong sense of what Imperial should look like after its restructuring, which was something they had to undertake in any case. 'What we didn't expect was that a global credit crisis, and all the other difficulties, would come along, and obviously this made the process considerably harder.' Not only were they, as an organisation, 'in need of our medicine, but the world, too, was going through a tough time'. From a staff perspective, it was crucial to communicate regularly with the employees to keep them informed of where the organisation was headed. Hubert stresses the importance of repeating the same message over and over; eventually it 'becomes inculcated very strongly' so that people start orienting their own actions accordingly and aligning their decisions with it. 'So, most important of all was the internal side of the matter.'

Hubert managed to achieve what few other people could have done; within a few years, Imperial was back on a winning path and once again a favourite among investors. What stands out for him when he looks back on his first years as chief executive?

He singles out 'the fact that we had to take huge decisions to create the right foundation for our group, and those things we did simultaneously. Normally you would do them one after the other.' He admits that those radical decisions were tough, 'but we chose a very good foundation and an excellent group of businesses as the basis of the group – the automotive industry and the logistics industry and related sectors. We also made our selection according to where there were good cash-flow streams, and opted for the type of businesses that have very good long-term prospects, both in the South African environment and globally.'

Under Hubert's leadership, Imperial is now making bigger acquisitions than ever before, yet he believes in their motto, 'Spirit of Entrepreneurship'. How does one foster that entrepreneurial mindset in such a large organisation?

Imperial is a business that consists of many small businesses, Hubert explains. 'We often refer to ourselves as a federation. If you look at the United States, for instance, it is actually made up of 50 individual states that all operate in accordance with a particular constitution, yet there is a lot of independence within the individual states and, in the case of Imperial, within the individual businesses.' If people are allowed that level of independence in their businesses and are genuinely in control of their circumstances, you can get the best out of them. 'This is the Spirit of Entrepreneurship,' he says, 'that we give people enough freedom so that they can truly realise their dreams within their business.'

I understand now why the Imperial board chose Hubert. What struck me during the interview, besides how comfortably he handled being on camera, is how he approached everything coolly, calmly and with logical judgement. His decisions are also taken in that light; it is clear that a bit of turbulence or an occasional TV camera won't put him off his stroke. I think Bill Lynch would have been proud of the bigger and stronger Imperial of today.

HUBERT'S LEADERSHIP PRINCIPLES

- High energy levels and good self-knowledge are the most important qualities of a senior leader in an organisation. In addition, a leader should be receptive to information and be willing to act on it.

- In Imperial, he appoints people who 'grasp an opportunity when they spot it and can also find new opportunities'.
- Be aware of trends in your industry and in your business.

IMPERIAL'S PRINCIPLES FOR SUCCESS

- A big transaction should never change the DNA of the business. By DNA he means 'the whole culture of a business – the things that motivate people, the way they go about their daily work'. They have never combined Imperial's entrepreneurial culture 'with a bureaucratic culture that could harm our dynamic way of doing things'.
- A big transaction should always be done for the right strategic reasons.

CHAPTER 16

Louis van der Watt

CO-FOUNDER AND CHIEF EXECUTIVE OF THE ATTERBURY PROPERTY
GROUP | *Interview broadcast on 8 February 2012*

Louis did his first property deals at the age of 11 and won the *Beeld/ Rapport* Young Entrepreneur award at 16. He studied at the University of Pretoria and qualified as a chartered accountant. In 1994 the 27-year-old Louis and Francois van Niekerk founded what is today the Atterbury Property Group. The group owns assets in excess of R10 billion, which include some of the country's largest shopping malls and mega-development projects. In 2009 Louis received the Christo Wiese Medal for outstanding entrepreneurship from the South African Academy of Science and Arts.

his interview was one of the most popular when it came to viewer numbers and feedback. Much of this could be attributed to the informal ease with which Louis handled the conversation. Louis grew up in an academic home; his dad, Professor Flip van der Watt, was a Theology professor at the University of Pretoria. Yet Louis had a passion for business and started doing property deals on his own at the age of 11. It sounds almost unbelievable, and I wanted to find out from him how his first transaction came about. He was in Standard 4 at the time, says Louis, and the concept of timeshare had just been introduced. When he looked at some of the lists that offered weeks for sale in timeshare schemes, he noticed that a certain week, during which the Transvaal schools had a holiday but not those in the rest of the country, was wrongly priced. It was being sold as a low-priced week while the price of all the other holiday weeks was high. 'I bought two of those weeks,' Louis recalls. 'I only paid a deposit, and a month afterwards a circular arrived saying that they had given the wrong price and that it was now double the amount. Then I sold them again, and that's how I made my first money.'

It must have been quite a shock for salespeople to do business with such a young client. Louis says he can still remember that, when he opened the door, they would usually ask whether his father was at home, assuming that their appointment was with him. 'Then my father would come around the corner and say, "No, no, just talk to that guy, it's him," and they would look utterly amazed, but after a while one got used to it.'

Louis studied Accountancy at university and qualified as a chartered accountant. While doing his articles, he befriended one of his audit clients, Francois van Niekerk from Infotech, who shared his interest in property. When Louis spotted an opportunity in Pretoria 'where land had become available – municipal land and some houses', he realised that it was 'very good land' and asked Francois whether he would be prepared to stand surety if they bought the property. Francois agreed. 'We did a few other property transactions as well before we came together and decided to start Atterbury, and that's how the property company was founded.'

It took five years before Louis appointed any staff at Atterbury. When talking about his subsequent success, he attaches a great deal of value to these first years; in his view, you need about five years to gain experience, 'to know what you're letting yourself in for'. He considers himself fortunate that they did developments during that time with people such as Louis Norval and Neno Haasbroek, from whom he learnt 'an incredible amount'. In those first years Louis did the books, rentals and project management, 'but I think it was necessary, because five years later you know exactly what kind of people you need in what positions', and he reckons that it helped them later to appoint the right people.

Not many individuals know exactly what they need from day one. As Louis puts it: 'I know very few people who can jump in and immediately do something right. I can't tell you how many mistakes we made in those five years, but five years later you start to understand.'

Today the group has property assets amounting to more than R10 billion, with well-known names such as Clearwater Mall, Garden Route Mall, Lynnwood Bridge and big developments in Midrand, among others, in their portfolio. They obviously have done many things right and successfully. One of the elements in which Louis believes is making staff shareholders, but according to a unique model.

In his opinion, there are three things Atterbury does differently from most other companies, and one of those is that they 'give the shares at the beginning'. Louis says he has learnt from experience that if someone has to work for his shares, 'he thinks for the rest of his life that the company owes him something' and that he is entitled to certain things. 'When you give it to the guy at the start, on the other hand, he is so grateful that, for the rest of his time at the company, he is not only loyal but also thinks that he owes the company something. So he constantly goes the extra mile.'

What irritated Louis immensely during his audit days was that the audit clerks worked until late at night and earned a pittance, 'and then you have some or other partner who leaves the office at four in the afternoon to play golf, yet he makes all the money'. The second thing they do differently at Atterbury is to 'reset' every five years. As Louis explains it, every five years they buy back all the staff's shares and then look at 'who the role players are at that moment. So the guy who is working hard at that point gets the most shares.' Nobody has a problem with it if you want to work less at some stage, but 'then you just have to accept that you will have fewer shares with the next "reset". Consequently, in the time that you work you get the shares you deserve.'

The third aspect that distinguishes Atterbury is that they don't attach too much value to qualifications. There are staff members who play roles that are totally outside of their discipline. The examples Louis mentions include someone who trained as a teacher and is now one of the top project managers, a woman who studied physical education and is now a director of the company, and CAs who don't even work in the financial department. 'But they all have one thing in common – they have incredible common sense and they are extremely loyal to the company.' They have a zeal for work without anybody having to police them, which Louis attributes to the fact that they are shareholders – 'it's important to them that this company should succeed'.

This belief in shareholding is so strong that it was extended to include friends and family. According to Louis, whenever some of the staff had a braai with friends who had attended the same school, the other guys would say, 'It's no use to us that you are so excited about the company; there's nothing in it for us.' So at some stage the Atterbury staff were told that their friends and family would be given a chance to buy shares in the investment company. 'The guys then all bought in, so all our friends are now shareholders, and I think those shares have almost quadrupled in the past five years. Now when we have a braai the whole group is happy, not just the one half.'

It is striking that many of the projects on which Atterbury embarks involve partners. Was this principle part of their strategy? You get people who build up their own company and then want to do everything themselves, says Louis, but because of time and staff constraints there are limits to what such a person can do. 'We have seen that with partners we can just grow so much faster, because you may suddenly get four or five opportunities simultaneously. But we also realised 'that it will only work if the partner also gets something out of the deal'. According to Louis, they often get calls from people who say that 'they have a piece of land, and that they have heard that we are good guys to work with' in developing it. He reckons this is due to the fact that they never do a transaction where the partner doesn't do extremely well too, and they don't mind if he remains a partner throughout. 'In the case of many of our developments, our partners are still shareholders with us, and you can call any of them – they're all very pleased with the partnership.'

Where Atterbury's business model differs from that of most other big property companies is that Atterbury develops the properties but then continues to own them afterwards. There are actually two companies within the group: Atterbury Property Holdings, the operational company that does the developments, and Atterbury Investment Holdings, the investment company. Louis regards it as a mistake on the part of other property developers that they don't own and manage their properties, as this weakens the inherent quality of the business. 'When the times turn against you, it's no use that you made all those profits,' he explains. 'It is then that you actually need a balance sheet to enable you to still borrow money and to continue generating income to carry you through that tough period.'

I wanted to find out from Louis why Atterbury is increasingly getting involved outside of South Africa. The first reason, he says, is 'merely diversification'; domestic opportunities are decreasing, and 'there are already too many shopping centres in every town'.

Secondly, 'the conditions in South Africa for companies like us to do business are simply becoming too difficult'. He finds it ironic that they do transactions in Namibia and Ghana in partnership with the governments of those countries, while the South African government shows no interest in such partnerships and actually makes it impossible for them to happen. Louis compares it to agriculture, where 'more and more farmers are starting to farm in the Congo or in Mozambique simply because the conditions are becoming too tough for them here, and I believe that is tragic'. Louis says he doesn't know what may happen in the next few years, 'but when entrepreneurs like us prefer to start developing in foreign countries, I think someone ought to take note of it and say, shouldn't we change our policy?'

In their annual reports, Atterbury stresses the social responsibility of companies. How do they fulfil this responsibility in practice? According to Louis, they have a 'soft spot for the Afrikaans-speaking people of the country'. When the company was founded, he and Francois created the Atterbury Trust, which provides bursaries to young Afrikaans people who cannot afford university studies. He reckons that they have already assisted about 250 students in this way, 'some of whom have since qualified as auditors and lawyers'. In addition, they pay the salaries of some teachers in schools in the western part of Pretoria, where they also support a nursery school. What their involvement comes down to, Louis says, is to help ensure that poor Afrikaners also have opportunities, 'because I think that the chances for them are diminishing in this country, and that is where we place our focus'.

I asked Louis about the rationale behind the group's decision to build a world-class 400-seat theatre in the Lynnwood Bridge development in Pretoria's eastern suburbs. Firstly, he says, through their interaction with some of the people involved in the arts they noticed that it was becoming increasingly difficult for them to stage Afrikaans productions in a state-subsidised theatre. Atterbury felt that if they built a theatre themselves, 'we wouldn't have to consult anybody about the productions we want to put on, and although it's not only for Afrikaans productions, it's nice to have control over what gets staged or not staged'.

A second reason that motivated their decision is that 'the whole culture of going to the theatre has actually disappeared'. People have stopped driving to the State Theatre because they feel unsafe in the city centre, so Atterbury situated the theatre in the eastern part of Pretoria, 'and every evening it's packed to capacity'. According to Louis, 'you can't believe how many people flock to the theatre and how this benefits the development. The theatregoers also eat out and spend money, so while there was a more noble idea behind the theatre, we're also making money from it, and that's how it should be.'

You know that you have talked to someone who knows his stuff when everything sounds very logical to you afterwards – this is usually an indication that the business model works and is well thought out. Like his Menlopark classmate Nicolaas Kruger, Louis was one of the younger people I interviewed; these two show that the younger generation is producing a healthy crop of entrepreneurs and business leaders. The country needs more Louis van der Watts!

PRINCIPLES FOR SUCCESS IN THE PROPERTY SECTOR

- Don't be too hasty in trying to make money – property is a long-term investment.
- 'Don't sell your assets and realise profits as quickly as possible, because the guys who survived the tough times were the ones who had a balance sheet that was strong enough to generate income.'
- You should never get into a position where you have to sell assets because you don't have a choice. 'When you're forced to sell something, you'll always come off second best in the transaction.'

- The principle of property as a long-term investment should become part of the culture of the firm. All the staff members should realise that 'building a balance sheet is more important. Even in their personal lives. First get that done before you start looking at things like expensive cars and other luxuries.'

CHAPTER 17

Altmann Allers

CO-OWNER AND EXECUTIVE CHAIRMAN OF GLASFIT

Interview broadcast on 15 February 2012

Altmann is an old boy of Paarl Boys' High, where his father was a teacher. He studied at Stellenbosch University and qualified as a chartered accountant. In 1996 he joined Glasfit, the company he would take over. Today Glasfit consists of a network of more than 130 fitment centres. Altmann is a co-owner of the Louisvale wine estate as well as co-owner and vice-president of the Golden Lions Rugby Union.

Our conversation started and ended with education. With a father who was a teacher, and other family members who are involved in the teaching profession, Altmann has a strong interest in education and believes that quality teachers and a sound education system are crucial to the development of people, communities and the country.

Many people can't get jobs today with a matric qualification or even a bachelor's degree, he says, and a solution may be to restore 'the quality of the matric'. Altmann refers to the role of teachers in society, which has shrunk over the years in a commercialised environment – 'they no longer enjoy the status they used to have'. In his view, we are currently 'sitting on a powder keg' because not enough good teachers are being brought into the system. 'We have to create teachers who are motivated, who want to do the work, and who realise that it's a long-term investment.' They only see the fruits of their labour at a much later stage and mostly don't even get any credit for it. Altmann feels strongly that teachers have a much greater part to play in society because so many resources are being managed poorly.

After his study years at Stellenbosch University, which included men's residence rugby and various social responsibilities, Altmann qualified as a chartered accountant. I wanted us to look at the point in his career when he joined Glasfit as its financial head. It was 1996, and six months later the company found itself on the verge of bankruptcy. Altmann admits that this came as 'an enormous shock' to him, particularly because Glasfit had been South Africa's unlisted company of the year in 1995. Their situation made him realise that many successful companies that make profit also 'make big management mistakes'. In Glasfit's case, it simply boiled down to the fact that 'the cash flow wasn't right'. The lesson he learnt from this, Altmann concludes, is that 'a profitable company isn't necessarily a successful company. A successful company is a company that has positive cash flow over a long period.'

In 2000 Altmann and other members of the management team decided to buy the company themselves. Why would one want to take over a near-bankrupt company? As Altmann explains it, the management team – himself, Brian Stolk, Jean Fouché and Barry Miller – had been working together for some time at that stage. They believed that Glasfit didn't really fit into the long-term strategy of the then holding company, and that they could do more with the company if they were independent.

The Glasfit Group has since developed into such a healthy business that they have expanded their activities and also act as a service provider for complementary businesses. I asked Altmann how they went about establishing Digicall, a cluster of businesses offering specialist skills in administration, claims processing and customer service. It was actually their 'electronic branch', he says, which was responsible for the administration of the Glasfit Group. They always thought they could do more with it, but didn't have the required expertise within the management team at the time. After they appointed Willem de Clercq as chief executive, however, he developed Digicall into a strong company in its own right, with less than 10% of its business coming from Glasfit. What they did with Digicall, Altmann reckons, is that they 'didn't force it'. They refined the basic systems that they used in Glasfit over time, and then 'applied them in other sectors outside the Glasfit Group and thus recruited external clients'.

Today the Glasfit Group has a national network of over 130 fitment centres. Why does their model work? According to Altmann, Glasfit Holdings 'basically provides the corporate management and the financial assistance while the owner behind the counter provides the entrepreneurship that is so important in a service organisation. It's really just easier for an owner to work longer hours than it is for a manager, and, at the end of the day, you get better client service.'

Altmann succeeded in transforming a virtually bankrupt company into a thriving business. He saw the opportunity within the shambles and grasped it. In general, though, he feels that people prepare themselves for an opportunity but fail to seize it when it comes up. Altmann elaborates on this by explaining that all of us get an opportunity at some or other time, yet we often let it go by. He refers to the many stories of people who say later: 'If only I made that investment at the time, or took that decision, or accepted that job.' Altmann reckons that the failure to seize opportunities can be attributed to fear. 'We aren't natural risk-takers, and it's perhaps in the Afrikaner DNA to be like that.' To the Americans, on the other hand, it is 'a normal event' to open and close businesses. In South Africa we spend so much time on starting a business, and Altmann believes that 'administrative red tape' is also an impediment. The result is that when an opportunity does present itself, it is as if we choose rather to stay within our safe cocoon than to take a chance.

Besides opportunities, what is his opinion on the role of luck in business? Luck does play a considerable role, Altmann says, in the same way that it often determines the result of a rugby match or a sports meeting. At times the referee's decision is in your favour, and on other occasions it is against you. That is how life and businesses work too, 'but I also believe that you can create your own luck'.

I wanted to get Altmann's views on doing deals and why one sometimes loses perspective during negotiations and takes rash decisions. He reckons 'it's a case of blood to the brain'. You get so excited that you forget about 'all the checks and balances you determined so carefully beforehand' and just want to clinch the deal with all your might. This is very dangerous, he says, because in the end you may decide to continue with the deal for the wrong reasons. When it comes to his own career, Altmann maintains that 'some of my best business deals I ever did were those I didn't get'.

Altmann was born and bred in the Western Cape. Yet he opted to get involved with the Golden Lions Rugby Union and even became the equity investor in the group. How did a Western Province supporter become so passionate about the Golden Lions? When he moved to the north of the country he was still a fervent Western Province and Stormers supporter, Altmann explains, but at some point you have to decide: 'Where are you really? Where is your little place in the sun?' After ten years he realised that his future and his family were in Gauteng, 'so I decided to start supporting the local teams and hence the Lions'.

Supporting a team is easy, but allocating a considerable part of one's capital to an investment in a sport union is something else. As an investor in the Golden Lions Rugby Union, what are Altmann's views on the administration of sport, and specifically of rugby? He believes that there are 'definitely deficiencies', which have to do with 'administrative structures inherited from the amateur era'. We moved into a professional era in the mid-1990s, Altmann says, 'but unfortunately many of the amateur structures survived at the administrative level'. Hence you find that 'many of the decisions in sports administration, and specifically in rugby administration, are taken by people who have been elected to positions. So you can understand that rugby politics now also comes into play. Decisions are taken that aren't necessarily the best rugby business decisions, and at the end of the day this has far-reaching consequences for rugby.' What is needed to raise the standard of administration, he reckons, 'is to get more and more professional people and professional companies involved in the administration of rugby'.

Does he believe one can make money from an investment in sport? According to Altmann, most people would say that it is not a very smart thing to do, but he doesn't quite agree. If 'we don't turn it around' and get to a situation where it makes financial sense to invest in sport, we should perhaps abandon the idea as soon as possible and return to the amateur era. He believes one can indeed make money from sport, but then 'you have to make sure that you manage it like a business and that you don't allow all these amateur/political decisions to affect your financial goals'.

113

In the course of the interview, Altmann highlights the small difference between 'almost winning' and 'almost losing' in a sporting context: the two are so close, and yet the outcomes are poles apart. There is nothing wrong with 'almost losing' matches; the problem arises when you 'almost win' too many matches. On the sports field as well in the business world, the difference may be small, but a series of 'almost victories' will never equal an 'almost defeat'.

We concluded the conversation by returning to education. Altmann cautions again that if South Africa doesn't address the challenge of quality education, we face the prospect of a powder keg that will explode in our faces – hence his approach of creating a fund for his alma mater with the aim of attracting and retaining quality teachers. If we fail to tackle this problem, will our children talk one day about how the new South Africa almost won?

ADVICE TO ENTREPRENEURS

- **Emphasise corporate governance and administration** – 'Many businesses today don't really have an idea of what their actual financial position is at a specific stage, for the simple reason that they didn't invest in administrative systems and good corporate governance is not applied. Eventually you end up with a very good business in the red.'
- **Always preserve your integrity** – 'This is an area we feel very, very strongly about. We believe that, at the end of the day, all you have is your name. It doesn't matter what product or service you sell. Ultimately, it is only about your name.'

CHAPTER 18

Elmien Scholtz

OWNER AND CHIEF EXECUTIVE OF BIO SCULPTURE INTERNATIONAL
Interview broadcast on 22 February 2012

Elmien studied beauty therapy and found that the South African market lacked quality nail products. After a fruitless search abroad for a product that could meet her standards, she returned to South Africa and opened her first beauty salon in Eastgate in 1989. She developed the Bio Sculpture range of nail products, which she marketed successfully in South Africa before starting to export in 1994. Today Elmien runs an international business empire from her headquarters in Clocolan in the Free State. Bio Sculpture exports to over 40 countries, with celebrities such as Jennifer Aniston and Victoria Beckham among her customers. Besides her many other accolades, Elmien was the South African winner in the Emerging category of Ernst & Young's World Entrepreneur Awards in 2011.

I wasn't quite sure what to expect when we were arranging the interview. All I knew about Elmien was that she is a local beauty therapist and entrepreneur who has received accolades for her products worldwide, from California and Scandinavia to Thailand. What stood out during the interview, however, was Elmien's absolute passion for her products and her business.

Where did her interest in nail products originate? While she was doing her beauty therapy training in Stellenbosch, Elmien says, she realised that, although nails were already a multibillion-dollar industry, there was still 'a big gap'. The products that were on offer were simply not satisfactory. 'You had a choice of heavy acrylics that were very difficult to remove, plastic nails that you could glue onto the nail, and of course nail polish, and these provided no protection for the nail.'

Elmien knew exactly what she was looking for, but her searches failed to deliver a solution that met her requirements. But this didn't deter her. I wanted to know how she felt when she returned from the United States without having achieved her objective, and that after selling her car to finance her trip. Initially she was disappointed, Elmien admits, 'but it also opened a big door for me. Remember, if I had found a solution I would probably still be using it today and only have the one salon, but because there was nothing it gave me the opportunity to develop the perfect nail system.'

Back in South Africa, Elmien got married, opened a beauty salon in Eastgate, and started developing her own nail product with a loan from her husband. She drew up a wish list of all the qualities she wanted to see in the ideal nail-care system, both as a customer and as a beauty therapist. After intensive research and development, the result was a user-friendly product that is also one of a kind. Her system was completely different from anything available in the beauty market. As Elmien puts it, 'Bio Scupture developed the world's first permanent nail colour' and 'the world's first gel extensions', along with a number of other 'firsts' in the industry.

Before long, Bio Sculpture was available not only in Gauteng but also in some of the bigger centres across South Africa. Her company reached a major milestone in 1994 when she started selling internationally. According to Elmien, Bio Sculpture was one of the first companies to start exporting after sanctions were lifted. Initially the product was introduced in foreign countries by South Africans who had emigrated during the 1990s. Nowadays they prefer to use local people to handle imports to a particular country, she says, 'but that was how we started'. Bio Sculpture offers people the opportunity to own businesses, and Elmien stresses that 'this is not just for the importer or the area manager'. Small businesses are mushrooming all over, 'and with last year's [internal corporate] census we discovered that there are already over 168 000 individual businesses where people make a living from Bio Sculpture and employ others as well'.

Today the product is available in over 40 countries. Was this her dream? Elmien confesses that she 'was so incredibly excited about this product. I just wanted to share it with everybody.' She always said that she wanted to see it available globally, but was also aware of the fact that you need to control your growth, 'otherwise we might have been in 140 countries by now'.

You have to make sure your product will work in the country to which you export it – especially when it comes to cultural differences. 'We have to adapt to the various cultures,' Elmien explains, and much research is done about a country before it joins Bio Sculpture. While certain things, such as their branding, 'may not be touched', they do allow importers considerable leeway to use branding that will work best in each country for growing and developing the brand.

It must give Elmien a great deal of satisfaction that her customers include global celebrities such as Katy Perry and Rachel Stevens. Yes, she says, they do have a long list of celebrities that use the product, but what appears to excite Elmien more than famous names is that their product 'is really meant for all women' and can satisfy any woman's specific needs, regardless of her occupation or cultural background.

I was fascinated by the fact that the head office of this globally recognised brand is in the modest surroundings of Clocolan in the Free State. According to Elmien, they initially moved to the town because her husband Carl, a veterinarian, wanted a large-animal veterinary practice, 'but it is also the lifestyle we prefer. We want to be here in nature and the land is important to us.' The country lifestyle 'brings balance' to their lives, she adds, because they are both very busy people.

I wanted us to move to the business philosophy side and to focus on what Elmien did right, unlike many other entrepreneurs that fail to make the grade. We started with the growth of the company and how it was financed. Elmien believes that no company, particularly when it is very young, can grow if it is burdened by 'financial pressures, high interest and debt'. Hence they opted for 'the slower and more stable route' of internal financing. They first focused on parts of South Africa and then, once the business was stable in those parts, moved on to the rest of the country. 'We then developed the business in the first foreign country with the funds and the profit of South Africa.' The business was developed in the second foreign country with the funds from the first, and that was the pattern they continued to follow. She reckons that their stable growth is 'one of the reasons why we are so renowned, because the foreigners have a lot of confidence in our brand'.

Throughout this growth process, however, she always put her products ahead of profit, and believes that this is a crucial principle for long-term success. 'If you're always just thinking money, money, money, you'll definitely never do research and development, because it's expensive.' When it comes to the development of a new colour, for instance, 'if you had to keep count of the number of dollars you're throwing into the rubbish bin, you would perhaps take a short cut or use something else that is cheaper, and then you'll never be the best. You'll never get that quality.' Elmien emphasises that you should focus only on the end product and on quality. 'With hard work, the money will come.'

As far as ideas and entrepreneurs are concerned, she feels that people with a good business idea sometimes hesitate unnecessarily and first wait for others to agree with them before taking action. 'If you always want to wait for someone else's approval he or she may end up doing it on their own,' she warns. 'So if you believe in something, just do it.' Referring to her own case, Elmien remarks that she is a woman and Bio Sculpture manufactures products for women. She knows what she needs, 'and if it's going to work for me it will work for the next woman as well, if such a product doesn't exist yet'. She believes that this principle applies in any field. 'If there is something that is not available in the market and that you need, the next guy needs it too. So don't wait.' Elmien reckons that there is 'still incredible potential' for expansion, growth and new entrepreneurs in South Africa. What often happens, however, is that people complain about a lack of something and see it as a problem instead of seizing the opportunity, 'making it their own and turning it into a success'.

During an interview, it is sometimes hard to get to the person and the business success; the product or service can dominate to such an extent that the conversation starts sounding more like a marketing or PR chat. In Elmien's case, the challenge was to keep her exuberant passion for her product in check. But, as the interview progressed, I realised that this passion is supported by strong business acumen and that the success of her business is most certainly not due to chance. Elmien is an entrepreneur of stature – the global market is the playing field on which she fulfils her passion.

ADVICE TO ENTREPRENEURS

- **Stay focused** – 'Stay positive and pray for wisdom.'
- **Learn from others** – 'It's better than having to suffer the consequences of your own mistakes.'

- **Persist with research and development** – 'It's very, very important that you stay ahead.'
- **Training** – 'Regardless of the product that you offer, it's only as good as the way in which it is used.'
- **Your people make your business** – 'By people, I mean your suppliers, your employees and your customers. You need to listen to them and hear what they have to say, because you can't do it on your own.'

CHAPTER 19

Louis Fourie

CO-FOUNDER OF CITADEL AND FOUNDER OF THE LOGIC FILTER

Interview broadcast on 29 February 2012

(GALLO IMAGES)

Louis, the son of a train driver, grew up in humble circumstances and 'on the wrong side of the tracks' on the East Rand. He obtained a master's degree in Economics at the then Rand Afrikaans University (now the University of Johannesburg) and was one of the first winners of the Sake24 Economist of the Year competition. In 1994 Louis became a co-founder of Citadel, which grew into one of South Africa's leading wealth management businesses under his guidance. After his retirement as executive chairman of both Citadel and the financial services group Peregrine in 2006, Louis founded The Logic Filter, an independent advisory business that offers life guidance and personal mentorship to young professionals and emerging business leaders.

I n the mid-1990s there were heaps of insurance broking firms that all offered basic financial advice. With their advice focusing mostly on life insurance products, they were more like traditional policy peddlers. Yet one of these companies managed to transform itself into a full-fledged financial services group specialising in financial planning and wealth management for affluent individuals. Citadel, of which Louis was a co-founder and later executive chairman, managed assets of more than R20 billion on behalf of their clients by 2012.

What did Citadel do differently from the rest of the companies in the same market? 'There was a window of opportunity around 1994,' Louis explains, on account of two things that happened in that period. Firstly, the pension fund dispensation changed, and 'for the first time people got full access to their retirement savings. They were used to a monthly budget for 40 years, and suddenly someone put a few million rand down in front of them and said, "Do with this money whatever you think fit – just remember, it has to last you for the rest of your life."' All at once there was a great demand for advice, and financial greenhorns faced many pitfalls.

The second opportunity that the 1994 era offered Citadel came in the form of the great number of civil servants who received severance packages, which again created a need for investment advice. But in the case of Citadel, these opportunities were only 'the first stride of the 100 metres', says Louis; the 'other 99' they had to run themselves. They built up the business in a systematic way and set themselves apart from their competitors by trying 'something different'. According to Louis, they said to themselves, 'Let's start by being transparent about payments.' From day one, therefore, 'we showed people exactly what they were paying for their investments, which was unheard of at the time'. Louis reckons that this was a breakthrough and something that is fairly rare even today, despite changes in legislation. Along with transparency with regard to fees, he emphasises a second aspect that distinguished Citadel: objective advice that was not linked to the product or the institution.

'The right advice was the advice. We built a model around it.'

I soon realised that Louis's interest lies in people and human behaviour. His clients were mostly highly successful people, so what, in his view, makes some individuals more successful than others? Louis talks about two types of success, the ephemeral and the sustainable. The first important thing that always struck him during his interaction with clients, he says, is that the 'sustainable success stories' were individuals who focused on only one thing once they reached their thirties. They didn't 'flit from one thing to another'. They experimented while they were in their twenties, but then decided what they liked and what they would try to perfect during the next 30 years. He describes such individuals as 'one-industry, one-approach people', something that also characterises the careers of people such as Warren Buffett and Bill Gates. 'They actually did only one thing in their lives; they immersed themselves in it and became really good at it.' The second salient characteristic of the 'sustainable success stories' was that they were organised individuals, not sloppy. 'They looked after their interests very well – and most of them also took good care of their lives outside the world of work.' And what is also very significant, he adds, is that 'they kept on the straight and narrow'.

I was interested in hearing more about Louis's views on the importance of decisions people take in their thirties and that play such a major role in their subsequent success. According to Louis, this was something that always struck him in his earlier career as he listened to the older successful clients during their conversations; they took crucial decisions in their thirties that put them on either the wrong or the right path. 'You don't realise this when you are in your thirties. You think you're merely continuing with your twenties, but every day we see examples on the front pages of newspapers of guys who do the same things at 35 that they did at 25. But the result is totally different at 35.' Louis stresses the fact that your thirties are 'an extremely sensitive time in your life' – this is usually the time when you have a young family or become a parent for the first time, and your career is moving into the fast lane. And in South Africa, if you are talented, you find yourself on a 'platform of big responsibilities' at an early age.

I wanted us to move from the topic of success to that of happiness. How does Louis see the relationship between the two, or are they the same thing? Louis feels strongly that society already starts grooming us for success from the age of about seven. You are told that 'if you follow the recipe for success, the rest of your life will work out too'. Everything that is invested in you is directed at success, 'especially if you're talented'; what is lacking, however, is that 'during that time not even an hour of your life is devoted to happiness'. There is a 'subtle promise' that people tend to cling to: 'If you become successful you'll be happy anyway, so don't worry about it.' As an economist, he was struck by the fact that many economists end up writing books about happiness in their old age. 'It's as if it took them a lifetime to grasp that that promise isn't true. That if you're successful, that is all that you are. You may have become a billionaire and your business may be massive, but your eyes can still be empty.'

And can money buy happiness? 'Money is a funny thing,' Louis says. 'All the research I have come across shows that money can indeed buy you that first bit of happiness.' Having to walk to work is not very pleasant, 'but a 1300 car already solves that problem'. But once you progress from the 1300 to a 3-litre engine, the difference between the two cars 'hasn't really added anything more to your personal happiness'. As Louis puts it: 'So serious poverty and serious disadvantages can be sorted out with that first bit of money, but no one knows that the marginal effect of more money diminishes rapidly. Most people believe that there is a linear relationship between happiness and more money, which is one of the reasons why guys almost work themselves to death. They're waiting for that promise to be realised.'

Nowadays Louis specialises in life guidance and mentorship to young professionals and emerging business leaders, with a view to helping them become more successful in all facets of their lives – not only in their careers. The aspect of believing in yourself and in your abilities cropped up in this regard, and I asked him about the fine line that there seems to be between self-confidence and arrogance. Louis describes arrogance as that point you have reached when you look in the mirror 'and see something much bigger than what is actually standing there'. Arrogance entails that you start looking down on other people, good habits and sound processes, and that you are no longer receptive to good advice. 'Arrogant individuals are surrounded by yes-men, but people who can really offer them good advice start shunning them, because it's an embarrassment – they always know better.' And ten years later you may end up in a terrible position, he adds, 'because you have become so used to your own voice'.

Throughout the interview it was clear that Louis had reflected deeply on success and happiness – he is truly passionate about not only making people successful but above all helping them to lead happier lives. It takes a wealth manager to realise that a successful life has more to do with happiness than it will ever be about money. I am going to look more closely at Louis's publications in future; his ideas simply make sense!

CAREER CHOICE ADVICE TO YOUNG PEOPLE

- Allow yourself more freedom in your twenties; regard it as an apprenticeship phase in your life, an opportunity to look around and try out different things in order to determine what you like.
- 'Don't rely too much on what you have studied as being the be-all and end-all; it's only a small building block in the total picture.'
- Take note of the things you are naturally good at, and of the technical field that interests you – that is where you will be naturally competitive for the rest of your life.

PRINCIPLES FOR SUCCESS IN YOUR CAREER

- Focus on one thing and do it extremely well.
- Surround yourself with the best people – good people in your personal life, and competent, committed people in your professional environment.
- Choose the best people in their field and give them space to reach their own heights.

PRINCIPLES FOR INVESTMENT SUCCESS

- 'Nothing beats a constant saving pattern.' It is not about the amount of money or the size of the salary: 80% of financial independence is determined by your constant saving pattern and 20% by the investment decisions.
- There is no such thing as a wonderful investment decision; it is about discipline over long periods.
- Don't become too fond of debt; many professionals 'spend away' their retirement on the cost of debt.
- Steer clear of flamboyant promises of high returns; if the return sounds too good to be true, then it is too good to be true.
- Make a success of your career and 'ensure through honest, specialised and thorough work that that income stream stays on your side throughout your life'.

CHAPTER 20

Thys du Toit

CO-FOUNDER OF CORONATION AND FOUNDER OF ROOTSTOCK
INVESTMENTS | *Interview broadcast on 7 March 2012*

Thys grew up in Bonnievale in the Western Cape, where he matriculated as the top pupil. He obtained a BSc degree in Agriculture at the University of Stellenbosch, followed by an MBA, which he gained with distinction. After starting his career in the financial sector, Thys co-founded Coronation Fund Managers with a few colleagues in 1993. He became the chief executive in 1996 and under his leadership Coronation grew into one of South Africa's largest and most successful independent fund managers. Today Thys serves on the boards of a number of companies and runs an investment management business, Rootstock Investments, which focuses on wealth management for affluent families.

was struck by the fact that Thys is still actively involved with the school he attended in the rural town of Bonnievale, and kicked off our conversation by asking him about a principle he likes to highlight when talking to the children: 'You are what you choose to be.'

What he means by this, Thys explains, is that you are not going to achieve exceptional success if you 'think small'. 'I think it was one of the American investment bankers who said, "Employ them poor, bright and with a deep desire to be successful",' he remarks. Thys believes that if people have that approach to life, 'they have a better chance of making it big'.

Besides having grown up in an agricultural environment, Thys lives in Stellenbosch, serves on the board of Pioneer Foods and was also the chairman of KWV, one of the leading wine and spirits producers in South Africa. So it does not seem strange that he initially decided to study agriculture. But how did he end up in the world of investments and fund management?

Apart from the fact that agriculture 'probably runs in the blood' of South Africans, says Thys, traditional career guidance at the time recommended that you should study for a BSc if you excelled in maths and science at school. It was only when he embarked on his MBA that he realised his real interest lay in investments, and that he wanted to focus on that field.

I wanted us to go back to the establishment of Coronation Fund Managers in 1993. Thys and his colleagues founded the company just before the advent of the new order and the democratic election of 1994, not exactly a time that many people would have considered ideal to start a business that is based on confidence. After all, investments are about confidence in the future and in the people who take the decisions. To understand their motives and the successful building of the business, I asked Thys about the reasons for their decision.

Although 'these things are always hard to pin down,' he says, there are a few aspects that stand out very clearly when he looks back. In

1993 he and four of his colleagues at financial services group Syfrets decided that they wanted to break away and start their own business, in which they would hold shares. Thys explains that at that time 'the big life insurers were, with all due respect, complacent'. They charged high initial commission fees and their investment returns were not good; 'this was a gap that we spotted'. He points out that Investec and Rand Merchant Bank also started in this period. 'In other words, the stage was set for the changes.'

Thys reckons that the opportunity created by the environment played a part in the success of their business, as well as 'that deep-seated desire to do your own thing and then, of course, teamwork'. According to Thys, 'the fact that we were so focused and were never distracted by other things' also contributed hugely to their success. 'We simply wanted to provide excellent investment management, and I believe it's being perfected even further by the current team.' In addition, they 'embraced the new South Africa' and at first focused only on pension funds, good investment management and low costs. In summary, Thys says, a combination of factors contributed to their success, but especially 'focus and that desire to succeed'.

What I noticed in the case of Thys, as well as that of many of the other business leaders, is the role played by change and something fresh. The fact that there were already big and well-established businesses in the market was not an obstacle; instead, it created the opportunity. While these companies operated in a particular way and stuck to their recipe, Thys and his colleagues realised that things could be done differently and better. This point of departure, of a different and innovative approach, cropped up repeatedly during the interviews.

Over the years, Thys and Coronation had to choose among investments in different companies. When he looks back, would he say that there are obvious signs by which one can tell a good company from one that is less good?

According to Thys, there is 'a very fine line between success and failure'. Obviously there are aspects such as industries, profit margins, people and many other elements that distinguish good companies from the others, but he often finds that there are 'tell-tale signals' by which you can judge that a company's focus is wrong. 'If the focus is on the head office, on the titles, on political corporate infighting, if it takes long for financial results to be released, if there is chaos with regard to production runs, if the distribution networks are undefined – these are all signs of a company that has question marks hanging over it.'

Thys was the CEO when Coronation Fund Managers listed on the JSE in 2003, and he stepped down at the end of 2007. How does one achieve a balance between building and listing a business on the one hand, and one's family and personal free time on the other?

Thys, who has been living in Stellenbosch for the past 23 years, believes work often becomes so all-consuming that it can take over your whole life. Recalling the 19 years during which he commuted to Cape Town while working at Syfrets and Coronation, he says: 'The days started at five in the morning and ended at seven in the evening, so you needed to have a supportive wife, you had to have a family that understands, you had to have a network at work and at home that supports you. At the end of the day, you yourself have to determine those demands and you have to know what their impact will be.' He has changed his life a bit since those days, Thys assures me; he has an office in Stellenbosch, travels much less than in the past, and 'tries to maintain a better balance'.

Given his highly successful career, I wanted to find out from Thys what he considers to be the most difficult decisions in the business environment. In his view, decisions that change the strategic direction of the business are the hardest. In Coronation's case, for instance, they had to 'fire' their partner and their single biggest client, Sage. And decisions about people are also tough, such as having to dismiss senior colleagues.

When I ask Thys for his opinion on the role that luck plays in success, he quotes golfer Gary Player: 'The more you practise, the luckier you get.' Thys concurs with this statement, and, in his view, it also highlights the importance of a long-term vision. 'Our careers are not a sprint, but a marathon; if you keep focusing on the same thing, gaps open up and that's when the luck emerges.'

What would he single out as key principles in business and in one's personal environment? In addition to those attributes that are often emphasised, such as a strong character and strong values, Thys says there are a number of things in the South African environment that are close to his heart. 'One of the things we need to do in South Africa is to create an environment for entrepreneurs, because entrepreneurs create jobs. No one else creates jobs. Entrepreneurs need two things – capital and human capital. Hence I feel very strongly about the development of human capital and the preservation of capital.'

After our conversation it was clear to me why Thys is regarded as one of the gentlemen of the investment world and is so sought after as a board member. What stayed in my memory was the sincerity that was evident in his replies, as well as the honesty of his advice.

ADVICE TO YOUNG PEOPLE

- First get yourself a job. There is no such thing as the 'ultimate' first job; once you are in a working position, other doors start opening for you.
- Choose your passion and follow it. 'In the days when I was young, you were supposed to become a doctor or a clergyman or an engineer.' Nowadays there is a much greater choice of occupations and professions; do something you are passionate about.
- Your working career stretches over 30 to 40 years – think big, but remember that it's a marathon rather than a sprint.

FINANCIAL-ADVICE PRINCIPLES

- **People are too conservative** – 'Property and shares are growth assets, and people stay too easily in cash. That's a mistake.'
- **A long-term horizon** – If your portfolio grows at 15% per year, it doubles every five years and R1 then becomes R64. 'They say it's not "timing of the market" that counts, but "time in the market". So the longer you can invest in growth assets, the better.'

CHAPTER 21

Pieter de Waal

FORMER VICE PRESIDENT OF BMW MOTORRAD IN NORTH AMERICA

Interview broadcast on 14 March 2012

Pieter hails from the Western Cape and studied Civil Engineering at Stellenbosch University. After a successful career as both racing driver and engineer at various motor companies, he joined BMW, where he later headed the group's motorcycle business, BMW Motorrad, in South Africa. As a result of his success in South Africa, he was appointed head of worldwide sales and marketing for BMW Motorrad in Munich. In 2008 Pieter became vice president of BMW Motorrad in North America, a position he held until his retirement in 2012.

The crime writer Deon Meyer told me at one of his book launches about an old motorcycle buddy of his, Pieter de Waal, who was turning the global motorcycle market on its head. With Deon's help I contacted Pieter, who was at that stage head of BMW Motorrad for North America, and we agreed that I would do an interview with him during his next visit to South Africa.

We decided to conduct the interview at a BMW motorcycle dealership in Centurion. Dirk, the producer of the programme, had suggested that we walk around among the motorcycles in the showroom, with Pieter stopping every now and again next to a particular motorcycle while we talked and recorded. But what we failed to take into account was that the workshop was right below the showroom; from five in the afternoon customers would collect their motorcycles after servicing and would, of course, test whether their engines were still in good working order. Fortunately, by the time the sound, lights and cameras had been set up, the motorcycles had all been collected and the workshop was quiet.

I realised from the outset that Pieter is someone for whom business is about passion. At an early stage in his life, he had to choose between his career and his passion. After he had been with Atlantis Diesel Engines for a few years, Pieter recounts, he was told that he would be groomed for a management position in the company, on condition that he stopped participating in motorsport. His racing was considered 'dangerous' and 'did not suit their image'. He had to reflect on the matter and give them an answer. At the same time, Delta was advertising a position for head of motorsport; Pieter applied 'on the spur of the moment', and got the job.

'I can still remember the day I walked into the office of the managing director of Atlantis Diesel Engines and told him that I had made my decision, but that I had decided my career would be in motorsport.' Pieter describes this as 'a turning point in my life, because, without really knowing it, I had chosen to follow my passion'. He had scarcely settled in at Delta when he got a call from Nissan, where he would spend many years as head of Nissan Motorsport. Eventually he got a call from BMW, 'asking me to work for them'.

How did it come about that Pieter, a motorsport fanatic, switched from BMW's car business to the company's motorcycle operations? Pieter admits that motorcycles did not really interest him at that stage. But when he joined BMW his position included motorcycles, which was 'a tiny division' at the time. So he felt duty-bound to obtain a motorcycle licence, 'and, once I started riding motorcycles, I discovered that this was a wonderful new world'. Motorcycling also became a shared passion for Pieter and his musician wife; previously, when he was still focused on motorsport, they had had few interests in common. From this 'wonderfully enriching experience', says Pieter, 'a vision was born', although he did not realise it immediately. 'The vision was to sell the lifestyle and not necessarily the motorcycle. The ideal was to create a world that would be so enticing that people would say, "Wow, I want to be part of this adventurous world of doing things, of exploring places," and they would almost incidentally buy a BMW motorcycle to gain entry into this world.'

When Pieter became head of BMW Motorrad in South Africa, the company was selling between 50 and 150 motorcycles per year. By the time he accepted the position in Munich as head of sales and marketing worldwide, BMW's motorcycle sales had increased to 3 000 units per year and their market share in South Africa was about 40% – the biggest in the world. This was an exceptional achievement by any standard, and I asked Pieter to explain the strategy that had underpinned this growth. Without a vision, he says, 'you don't really give a company the opportunity to grow in a focused way'.

Pieter had his vision of linking the BMW motorcycle to a lifestyle, 'but there were a number of obstacles'. Firstly, he knew that customers like himself, 'in other words, 40-plus, successful, probably professional people', wanted a sales experience that was tailored to their status in life. Secondly, there was the red tape involved in obtaining a motorcycle licence, as well as the difficulty associated with learning how to ride a motorcycle on dirt roads. 'Hence we felt that, apart from creating a place where customers would feel at home, we also had to make it easy for them to get a licence and to learn how to ride off-road. All of this fitted under a lifestyle umbrella.' They decided to build a lifestyle centre in Midrand, but, according to Pieter, this also took some doing. 'There was of course no business case for this, and at first the board would have none of it, but I was so convinced it would work that I didn't give up.' He eventually got the go-ahead from the board, and the centre was an immediate financial success; in the first year, more than 70% of all motorcycle sales in South Africa came from the BMW Lifestyle Centre.

After a stint in Britain, Pieter was appointed head of BMW Motorrad's global sales and marketing division based in Munich, the first non-German to reach this level. How does one approach the challenge of such a position in an international company? Pieter singles out two aspects. Firstly, it is 'important to see the big picture' and to make sure that you understand where you want to be in the future. 'So that's the first thing – keep the vision for the future simple and ensure that everyone who reports to you knows what is expected of them.'

Secondly, he says, it's about people. If you find yourself at the helm of such a large organisation, comprising not only the head office staff but also all the staff members in the more than 70 countries who contribute to sales, 'it's vital to have the right people in the right positions'. Pieter also emphasises the importance of delegation in a company of that size. 'I always kept harping on the same string, which was where we wanted to be in the future, and I relied on my people to get us there.'

I was curious to know what it felt like to do business in a foreign language, and what Pieter learnt from the experience. According to Pieter, he soon realised that 'while it was one thing to conduct a social conversation in German, it was something totally different to try and put your view across in a boardroom when people are perhaps not quite getting your point, or are unwilling to do so'. This led to frustration on his part – 'I always felt that I was on the back foot.' The lesson he learnt from this, however, is something he still applies today: 'When you're doing business with people who are speaking in a second or even a third language, it's very important not to confuse the knowledge they possess with the way in which they express that knowledge.'

In Pieter's view, South African businesspeople 'don't have to take a back seat to anyone else. If you're a South African and you stand out in your working environment in South Africa, you're probably also on the level of the best in the world.'

In 2008 Pieter was appointed vice president of BMW Motorrad in North America, which includes the United States, Canada and Mexico. His explanation of the logic behind this move made me realise why the company decided to put their best man in charge of this crucial market. In contrast to the car industry, which enjoys the advantage of emerging markets such as China, India and Russia, Pieter says, similar markets don't exist on 'the motorcyle side'. In the East, motorcycles are used as a cheap mode of transport – these are not the kind of motorcycles that BMW sells. A critical examination of possible growth points led them to the conclusion that BMW Motorrad had been focusing mainly on Europe and to a lesser degree on the rest of the world, with only 10% of their sales coming from America at that stage. This was totally out of sync with what most of the other manufacturers were doing. 'So it was clear to us,' Pieter says in summary, 'that if we could crack the American market we would have a long-term growth process. If we couldn't manage to do that, we would actually be snookered.'

In reply to my question about BMW Motorrad's subsequent progress in this market, Pieter remarks that 'in the past four years we have doubled our market share in America and built on our profit'.

On two occasions in his life, Pieter sacrificed money and promotion in order to follow his passion. Looking back on his career, he believes that in both cases this was the right decision. Initially he had started out as a civil engineer, but he didn't like the work and wanted to get into the motor industry instead. At Mercedes-Benz he began 'working on the line' and enjoyed it tremendously. 'I also discovered I was the only guy who enjoyed it, because for the workers on the line it was only about money, and for the engineers sitting in the offices it was just a theoretical exercise.' The second time he made this choice was when he opted to pursue his passion for motorsport instead of climbing the corporate ladder at Atlantis Diesel Engines. This conviction about the importance of one's passion is what gave rise to Pieter's philosophy of life.

I concluded the interview by referring to Deon Meyer's remark that Pieter has irrevocably changed the global motorcycle market. According to Pieter, one needs to keep in mind that Deon is a writer of fiction and 'exaggerates terribly'. 'But if I did make a contribution,' he adds on a more serious note, 'it was probably in trying to sell a lifestyle instead of a motorcycle or a product.' This approach worked in South Africa, he says, 'and I hope it will work in America as well. It's difficult and it takes a long time, but when it works you have a product that others can't imitate.'

What will stick in my memory is the absolute passion with which Pieter, before and after the interview, described every motorcycle in the showroom and the joy you can derive from them. His passion for the lifestyle is bound to sell many more BMW motorcycles in future!

PIETER DE WAAL'S PHILOSOPHY OF LIFE

'When you do that which you really enjoy doing, you don't mind doing
it all the time. When you do something all the time, you become good
at it and when you are good at something, people want your services.
When people want your services, it is called success and when you are
successful, the money follows. But it doesn't work the other way round.
First comes passion, then money.'

CHAPTER 22

Nicolaas Kruger

CHIEF EXECUTIVE OF MMI HOLDINGS

Interview broadcast on 21 March 2012

Nicolaas excelled in mathematics at school and wanted to work in a field where he could use his mathematical and analytical abilities. After studying Actuarial Science at Stellenbosch University, the 23-year-old Nicolaas joined the Momentum life insurance company as an actuarial assistant in 1991 and qualified as an actuary the following year. At the age of 29 he was appointed chief actuary, and in January 2009 he became the chief executive of Momentum at the age of 41. In 2010 Nicolaas was appointed the first chief executive of the new MMI Group, which was born from the merger of Momentum and Metropolitan.

Our conversation began with the advice Nicolaas received in his matric year from Sanlam's Marinus Daling, who convinced him that actuarial science was the right direction for him and that it 'provided a very good platform for a business career'. Looking back on his student years at Stellenbosch, Nicolaas remarks that initially 'you don't really know what you're letting yourself in for' when you opt to study actuarial science. The actuarial students had to slave away in the library while many other students had time for social activities, but 'it was worth it' in the end. One should keep in mind, he says, that the actuarial profession is extremely specialised and attracts few students. When he completed his studies 20 years ago, there were only 320 actuaries in South Africa. 'Today the number has grown to about 820, but it's still very low compared to other professions.'

After the interview, I talked to one of his former lecturers at Stellenbosch, who told me about the time that Nicolaas's classmates came to see him to ask why, despite their hard work, they never managed to beat Nicolaas when it came to tests. The lecturer's reply was succinct: Nicolaas not only works very hard, he just happens to be very clever as well!

After completing his studies, the 23-year-old Nicolaas started working at Momentum in 1991. At the age of 29, he was appointed chief actuary. What stands out for him when he looks back on the Momentum of 1991 and how it has grown from that time to the MMI Group of today? To put that growth trajectory into perspective, Nicolaas says, one should consider that 'the MMI Group of which Momentum now forms part makes a profit of almost R3 billion per year. It now takes the MMI Group just two working days to make the profit that Momentum made in a whole year 20 years ago. So it's been phenomenal growth over time.' According to Nicolaas, this growth trajectory started in 1992, when Rand Merchant Bank acquired Momentum and 'helped to establish the right culture'. The plan was that they should grow through a combination of organic growth and corporate transactions. Among the many corporate transactions Momentum concluded over the years, he highlights four in particular: 'it started with a transaction with Lifegro, then later a transaction with Southern, then the one with Sage, and of course more recently the merger between Momentum and Metropolitan.'

Nicolaas had the privilege to be exposed to three of the most successful businesspeople in South Africa, which contributed much to his own development. Much has been written about the achievements of Paul Harris, GT Ferreira and Laurie Dippenaar, and I asked Nicolaas what he recalls in particular about working with them. They are 'of course exceptionally successful entrepreneurs', he says, 'but they also complement one another very well'. According to him, the principles he learnt from this trio are quite simple: 'The first principle is a very solid and sound value system. Integrity takes precedence in everything you do, and your reputation is incredibly important.' Along with this, they have the ability to assess innovative opportunities, to spot business opportunities and to pursue the right ones. Laurie Dippenaar, in particular, was closely involved with Momentum and served as the company's chairman for many years. 'We obviously learnt an enormous amount from him – his long-term vision, his leadership, but also his sound value system.'

Throughout the interview, I was conscious of the fact that I was speaking to a highly intelligent individual. Yet when Nicolaas talks about advice that has made a difference to his life, he singles out Hillie Meyer, a former managing director of Momentum. Hillie explained to Nicolaas that he had to work at 'being able to convey a complex financial problem, or a complex financial structure, in a simple way that makes business sense'. I wanted to know why Nicolaas attaches so much value to this principle. In his view, it is extremely important for professionals, such as engineers, accountants and actuaries, 'to acquire the ability to explain their complex world to decision-makers in accessible language, because in that way justice can be done to their complicated work'. He recalls specifically that they put much effort into explaining to the board of Momentum how an insurer makes its profit, which was something that few people outside the ranks of the actuaries understood at the time. Such explanations 'help a board to take good business decisions'.

The modern trend is that people stay with a company for a few years and then move on. One seldom finds any more that someone joins a group, stays on and then, 20 years later, becomes chief executive of the same group. In his case, Nicolaas reckons one possible reason is that he is part of 'the Generation X people, who are much more loyal to their employers and perhaps tend to stay longer at the same place', in contrast to the young people of today, who like variety, move around more easily in search of new opportunities, and 'are just much more open to career opportunities'. But the main reason he stayed with the same group, he believes, is that it is a very dynamic group that has changed a lot over the years. Momentum had a few hundred employees when he started working there; today the MMI Group has more than 16 000 employees. Initially they were involved only in South Africa, and today they also do business in 12 other African countries as well as in the United Kingdom. 'The group has changed so much and so many new opportunities have been added that it's not really the same group as the one in which I started.'

Nicolaas's life does not only revolve around figures; in his free time he farms rare and endangered game species on a family farm in the Karoo. As he puts it, 'you can't work the whole time' and you need to have other interests too. They strive to run the farm on sound business principles, as well as on a natural and environmentally friendly basis, while simultaneously inculcating a love for the Karoo in the family and ploughing something back into the community. 'You are the steward of the farm that has in fact only been lent to you, and you want to leave it to your descendants in a better condition.'

During our conversation, I was constantly aware of the fact that I was talking to an exceptionally gifted individual with a strong value system – the kind of guy one would like to do the important sums. Fortunately he also saw it as his duty to explain to me how he arrived at the answers!

KEY ADVICE ABOUT INVESTMENTS

- Learn to live within your financial means as soon as possible. Even as a student – make sure that your expenses don't exceed your income.
- Start saving as early as possible in your career. 'Only one out of 20 individuals in South Africa saves enough for their retirement so that they can retire comfortably.'
- From early on, get a good financial adviser who can advise you about investing in such a way that you beat inflation over time.

BASIC MISTAKES THAT INVESTORS SHOULD AVOID

- Temptations that come your way in the form of very attractive investment opportunities that sound too good to be true. 'There is no such thing as an investment scheme that can make you rich overnight. All those schemes have some or other problem, so that over time they prove not to have been a good investment.'
- Concentration risks: having too much money in a particular place and 'putting all your eggs into one basket'.

CHAPTER 23

Johann Vorster

CHIEF EXECUTIVE OF CLOVER

Interview broadcast on 28 March 2012

After graduating with a BCom degree from the former Rand Afrikaans University, Johann worked as an auditor while completing his honours degree through Unisa and qualified as a chartered accountant in 1987. He obtained an MBA degree from the University of the Witwatersrand and worked in the manufacturing sector before joining Clover in 2000. In 2006 Johann was appointed chief executive, at the age of 41. Under Johann's leadership Clover listed on the JSE in 2010, and today the foods and beverages group has a market value of around R3 billion.

The interview with Johann was actually very easy. Apart from having more than enough to talk about, he was enthusiastic about Clover and proud of what they have achieved, particularly the value that has been unlocked for dairy farmers in the process.

Our conversation started with his background as a chartered accountant and the value it has added to his career in the business world. Johann reckons that it proved to be 'an enormously important' qualification for him, although he didn't work in the auditing industry for very long. He emphasises 'the financial knowledge you acquire, the background of how to analyse companies and do appraisals, and basically the conservatism it teaches you – how to determine risks'. When he started as an auditor and had to look at companies, he was struck by 'the creativity that chief executives can bring to a business' and 'immediately my mind was set on the sales and marketing side'. After three years at the Receiver of Revenue he decided to do an MBA, which he describes as 'a fantastic experience' because one studies the financial aspects of a business along with 'marketing, labour relations and all the other things'.

After completing his MBA studies, Johann wanted to work in the business world instead of returning to a financial environment. He joined East Rand Plastics, where he gained experience in turning around companies that were under financial pressure. The group started buying companies where they spotted opportunities. According to Johann, he 'eventually found a niche in companies that were struggling a bit, that needed cash and so on, and we ended up acquiring about 23 companies'. This led to the creation of Astrapak, which became a listed company. Johann was financial director of the company for about two years, and 'then luckily I was able to find my way back to the management side'.

His time at Astrapak was 'an immense training school' for him, as a result of which he joined Clover in 2000 as financial director. 'At that stage Clover was also going through a difficult time because they were undercapitalised, and I reckoned that if I could manage to do it for smaller companies why not try to do it for a larger company too.' Johann remarks that he 'had always been thrown in between the finances and the general management', but what you see from 'the financial side of a company' is of enormous value to you at a later stage when you have to manage a company.

Before we discussed his experience at Clover, I wanted us to touch on the beginnings of the group that is known as Clover today. Its history goes back to 1898, when a group of farmers at Mooi River in Natal established a butter factory that was run on cooperative principles. It was later known as National Co-operative Diaries (NCD). The name Clover was added in 1994, and in 2003 the cooperative society was converted into a public company. This conversion was a key element in Clover's growth, and I asked Johann what had necessitated the move. After 1994, he explained, funding for cooperatives from the Land Bank and other banks started to dry up. Wherever cooperatives exist in the world, the major constraints they have to contend with are their lack of capital and their access to capital. Hence it was 'a crucially necessary step' to give Clover 'the form of a company with independent directors'. But at that stage Clover had only undergone an outward change. 'It had not yet undergone a change of heart.' How they arrived at this change, Johann says, is 'the success story'.

In Clover's case, the conversion was essential, but I wanted to find out from Johann whether there was, in his view, still a place for the cooperative business model. Most definitely, he says. In Germany and a number of other European countries, some of the largest companies or organisations are cooperatives. 'Why is a cooperative such a wonderful thing? Because it creates assets. It's an incredible asset. If you look at NCD, it was an asset that had been built up by farmers over a period of 100 years. It's an asset-rich company that has not always been profitable, but I think we're now on the way to that. That's why a cooperative is so valuable: it builds assets.'

In the run-up to the listing of Clover on the JSE in 2010, the delivery rights of the dairy producers had to be converted into shares. Why was this change so important? As a cooperative builds up assets, Johann says, it becomes a target for takeovers. You protect the company against this by saying that 'those who own the company must also be able to deliver to it. So you keep it within the farming community.' Therefore the delivery rights 'were really just a poison pill against a takeover. But you can't have a poison pill against takeovers on the one hand and bring in new shareholders on the other. So it was vital to delink the milk delivery agreements from the shares, and this was the success we achieved in the end – managing to convince the producers, our farmers, that they had to cut that final knot in the process.'

Johann regards the listing as a highlight in the development of the group. In reply to my question as to why this was such a significant milestone, he explains that while they had had plans for growth and improvement for a long time, 'we just never had access to enough capital'. They increasingly had to resort to debt, 'which was very expensive commercial debt'. Accordingly they started lagging behind in areas such as technology, IT and vehicles. The listing was therefore an 'immensely positive' boost for the company. You could feel the buzz as you walked along the corridors, according to Johann. 'Suddenly we had R600 million in the bank, the debt had been repaid, and people were planning.' It felt to him as if he had only been working at the company for a year and a half, 'because it was a new company'.

To him, 'one of the most important things about the success story' was the value they managed to unlock for the farmers who had built up the cooperative. 'Between 13 and 14 December 2010 our producers became R1.3 billion richer, which I consider a phenomenal success story because the money went to the right people.'

According to Clover's business model, the group stresses that they have moved from the supply-driven company of the old days to a demand-driven business. What does this strategic shift in emphasis mean? As Johann explains it, since a cooperative is established mainly for the purpose of 'working away' the members' products by marketing, selling or distributing them, you have no control over what comes into your company. In the past, producers could deliver as much milk to them as possible, 'and we had to work it away'. Hence you end up being 'something of a spectator when it comes to your own income statement', because you receive varying quantities of milk from month to month and you don't always have the infrastructure to deal with it. 'We knew that no investor would invest in such a cyclical company if we couldn't offer him steady profits.'

In 2006 Johann informed the producers that the company would become demand-driven. 'In other words, we will only take in the milk that we can sell profitably; the rest of the milk you will have to sell elsewhere, or we enter into a contract with you once a year to say how you want to grow, and then we will look for other markets for that milk.'

Throughout the interview, Johann refers to the role of the farmers and the relationship between Clover and the milk producers. When I ask his opinion about this relationship, he stresses its interdependent nature. The quality brand that Clover has today 'starts on the farm, with how they look after their cattle'. To Clover, the farmers' contribution is a vital input that ultimately gives the brand its value, 'and that's why it's crucially important to us to have a very close relationship with these producers'. Clover, on the other hand, 'gives them growth. They are equally dependent on us, because the value of what they do on the farm is of course the value of their land.' Everyone always thought that the relationship 'existed as a result of the quota and the shares that were linked, but now we've seen that they are still just as loyal 16 months later. The relationship still works and we still have the quota system in place.'

Johann became chief executive at the young age of 41. How did he deal with this challenge, especially in the more conservative and traditional agricultural sector? He reckons that he was fortunate in being able to surround himself with 'very good people who gave me the necessary experience and support', but admits that, during the first 18 months, he felt there was 'something of a wait-and-see attitude as to whether this youngster was going to make it'. He refers to the enormous pressure on him to make his mark, 'to achieve successes as soon as possible and to celebrate them'. Not bragging about the achievements, he adds, 'but you have to tell the people that we managed to do these things and that we did them together. In that way you take them with you, and then later it all comes together.'

In his remarks about success, Johann emphasises that a company should have a narrow focus, and, in the case of Clover, he highlights the brand as a focal point. He explains his single-focus approach with reference to 'the limited resources'. In his view, you should select four or five things in a business that you are good at. The rest you can outsource. This approach has meant that Clover can focus on what they want as the ultimate goal, 'and that is the brand that we have to expand'. According to Johann, the Clover brand is 'much bigger than just dairy. It can be expanded much further. It is such a strong brand, which is supported by our distribution channels. Therefore I see a lot of benefits in having a single focus.'

He elaborates on this principle by saying that things do not happen by themselves. You must have a vision that is conveyed continuously, 'and then you need to get to work to put those things in place'.

Johann and Clover are situated squarely within the South African agricultural industry. On the one hand, there is the demand for land, and, on the other, are the pressures on food security. When I ask Johann for his opinion on the land question, he firstly places it in a global perspective. Clover's New Zealand partner Fonterra, the 'single largest exporter of milk or dairy products in the world', estimates that, by 2019, the world will need 'another six Fonterras to meet the demand for dairy products, given the rate at which China and India and other countries are developing'. As far as South Africa is concerned,

Johann refers to parts of the country where the available land and water are not being utilised optimally and reckons that there are many opportunities for dairy farmers. Their producers are working closely with the government to look at ways in which the land issue can be tackled and partnerships can be formed. In Johann's view, there is a need for 'a bit of a sanity check in this whole thing'. He believes that people should be realistic in their expectations about the value of the land, and that the process has to be accelerated because uncertainty prevents people from investing in farms.

After our conversation I agreed with Johann that there are few examples of cooperatives that were converted into companies in which the biggest winners were the members of the cooperative; in the case of Clover, the winners were the country's dairy farmers. To me, the salient feature of the interview was Johann's consistent faith in his farmers and his conviction that the future of Clover and that of the farmers are inseparably linked.

BARRIERS TO PROGRESS

- **Ego** – 'We can achieve much more if we stand together.'
- **Resistance to change** – Along with ego, this 'often gets in the way of good, sound business principles'.

CRITERIA FOR APPOINTMENTS AND PROMOTIONS

With a smile, Johann listed his three criteria promptly and succinctly:
- He attaches great value to loyalty.
- The person must be a team player.
- Trainability: the person must be able and willing to acquire additional skills.

CHAPTER 24

Ina Paarman

BUSINESSWOMAN AND FOUNDER OF PAARMAN FOODS

Interview broadcast on 4 April 2012

As a home economics teacher and later as a lecturer, Ina also wrote food columns for newspapers and was food editor for a women's magazine. The first step on the road to what Ina Paarman is today was her decision to start a cookery school in a converted garage at her home. The first Ina Paarman product, seasoned sea salt, was produced here. The Paarmans took a loan on their house to finance the publication of Ina's first cookbook. In 1990 the food company Paarman Foods was born when Ina's son Graham joined the family business. Today, eight cookbooks later, Ina Paarman products are sold in 16 countries and the company provides employment to more than 200 people.

The more research I did about the woman behind this truly South African product range, the more I was struck by her remarkable story. Ina Paarman has succeeded in establishing her name and persona in our kitchens as emblematic of excellent food.

We met for the first time about 30 minutes before the interview at Ina's Constantia kitchen in Cape Town. I realised right from the start that I was talking to an exceptional woman: elegant, professional and a formidable businessperson. It turned out to be one of the most memorable interviews because one could sense her sincerity; everything she said came straight from the heart.

I started our conversation with her decision to sacrifice the security of a job and a salary cheque in order to set up her own cookery school. The person who inspired her to take the risk of starting her own enterprise was 'definitely my mother', Ina says. 'She was also the one who told me, "My child, you're too clever to work for the government, why don't you start your own thing?" Then she gave me R4 000, and we got going.'

At first, the cookery school struggled to get off the ground. Ina attracted few pupils, and 'it was very hard to let clients know that I was now in business'. But starting the school was definitely 'the right thing at the right time' because it met a need. According to Ina, the introduction of the metric system was causing confusion at the time: 'suddenly people were unsure about pounds and grams, Fahrenheit and Celsius' when it came to cooking and making sense of recipes.

Ina started her career as a home economics teacher, and I gained the impression that she has remained a teacher at heart. The urge to help people improve their knowledge and skills is still at the centre of her books and products. The most wonderful thing about teaching, she says passionately, 'is that you can set off a spark in children's heads. That you can inspire them to start teaching themselves. Then you yourself don't have to work so hard, you just have to convey the message of what the knowledge can actually mean to them.'

153

The first Ina Paarman product, which was based on a recipe of her grandmother's, was created during this cookery school period. I wanted to find out whether this had been a planned next step, but, as Ina explains, it happened almost incidentally and more out of necessity. She had taken on a few workers at the cookery school to do things such as washing dishes. Mindful of her mother's advice that 'the best thing one can do is to create employment for others', she couldn't bear to send them home during the school holidays and looked for something to keep them occupied. 'So we started making the seasoned sea salt, and I really believe it was a sign that we were on the right track.'

The next big step in the building of the Ina Paarman brand was the decision to write and publish a cookbook. Ina couldn't find a publisher who was interested in the project, but this didn't deter her. The Paarmans took out a loan on their house and Ina published the book herself. 'I was on my knees every day, praying that it would work and that I would be able to repay my home loan, because my husband had cast his eyes heavenwards and said, "How can you mortgage the roof over our heads to try and sell a cookbook?"' To her great relief, the book was a hit; Ina reckons the tips she added in the margins as a result of her teaching experience, coupled with Stanley Pinker's illustrations, contributed to its success. 'But those first four months were really nerve-wracking – my stomach still gets in a knot when I think back – as I waited to see whether or not the book would sell.'

The Ina Paarman food products we all know today had their start in 1990 with the establishment of Paarman Foods, the manufacturing arm of the business. Ina's younger son, Graham, who was completing his BCom degree at Stellenbosch at the time, had proposed to her that they expand the family business: 'Mom, I can do sums and you can make food.' Today they export to 16 countries and are renowned as a brand that is associated with quality. While Ina concentrates on recipe development, Graham manages the business.

When I ask her about highlights on their road to success, she singles out Graham's entry into the business – 'he's a born entrepreneur' – and the nature of their teamwork. 'When you have a really bright, talented, hardworking child, you shouldn't let him work for other people. Let him join the family business.' Ina believes that partners should have different attributes and competencies so that they complement each other, and she regards their business as 'the ideal example' of successful teamwork. Her late husband also played a role in the business. To Ina, one of the major benefits of involving your family in your business is that you don't have to contend with 'that split' between your work and your family interests. 'I've always been a workaholic,' she confesses, 'so now I could be a workaholic without feeling guilty.'

The Ina Paarman website is visited by over two million people per month. Why is it so important to her to respond personally to as many queries as possible? In the first place she wants to know how her customers think and what their needs are, Ina explains, but it also gives her great pleasure to share new recipes with people and talk to them on an individual basis. And 'of course people appreciate the fact that you take the trouble to reply to a letter personally'.

Ina is passionate about quality and reckons that South Africans are too easily satisfied with mediocrity. 'I believe that there is always a market for quality. I believe in standards. You know, I'm too old and I've been in the business for too long to be content with second best. For me, it has to be right or otherwise you leave it,' she adds proudly.

How does it make Ina feel to walk into a supermarket and see her products on the shelves? It's like looking at your children, she says. 'You're obviously aware of their good qualities, but you can't help noticing that their shoelaces are undone and their shirts aren't tucked into their trousers.' Instead of only doing her own shopping, she ends up rearranging her products on the shelves if they have not been displayed neatly enough. She admits that it gives her 'such a good feeling' when customers come past and put any of her products in their trolleys. 'I always thank them for their support because, at the end of the day, it's the person who takes the product from the shelf that determines the success of a business.'

Celebrity chefs have become a cultural phenomenon, but Ina believes she owes her success to the very fact that she is not a chef or a celebrity cook, merely a good home cook who understands the needs of her customers. As a former technikon lecturer, she had to make 'a shift in emphasis' when she started teaching adults at her cookery school. 'They don't care whether they use the correct method or not, since they don't have to pass an exam – they want something that looks glamorous, that is quick to prepare, and that will take their guests' breath away and make them say, "Wow, you're a wonderful cook!"' Once again she gives her mother credit for the valuable advice she gave her at the time to do a cookery course in France and to observe how such courses were presented there.

I reflected on the interview afterwards, while driving back to the airport, and it occurred to me that businesspeople could benefit from what housewives across the country have known for a long time: you may safely follow what this petite lady recommends; it will work just as well in the boardroom as in the kitchen!

PRINCIPLES FOR SUCCESS

- Every person is responsible for their position. 'I don't believe at all in the victim mentality. I don't believe in thinking back to everything that went wrong in your childhood – it's in the past. It's water under the bridge.'
- It is everyone's duty to create their own luck. 'You make your own luck and you work at it. It doesn't drop from the sky. You have to make it happen.'

ADVICE FOR YOUNG PROSPECTIVE COOKS

- Don't be blinded by the glamour aspect of the profession. 'Every profession has its share of utterly boring, repetitive, exhausting work. My grandmother used to say that life is like yellow rice: mostly dry rice, and occasionally you find a raisin. You can't just pick out the raisins from the work. You have to be prepared to eat the dry rice too.'
- Make sure that you get a good scientific background, 'so that when a cake flops, you can understand why it flopped and are able to explain to someone else what to do to correct it. If you're only capable of making food according to the recipe, you still don't know why things turn out right or wrong.'
- It is the technical knowledge that determines whether you will be really successful. 'The glamour bit, that's easy to pick up, but if you have the intellectual capital behind the fine cuisine, it turns you into something that I believe is of priceless value.'

CHAPTER 25

Dr Christo Wiese

CHAIRMAN OF PEPKOR AND SHOPRITE

Interview broadcast on 11 April 2012

Christo studied Law at Stellenbosch University and joined Renier van Rooyen's retail chain Pep Stores in 1967. He left the group after seven years to practise as an advocate at the Cape Bar. In 1981 he rejoined Pep Stores, this time as the majority shareholder and executive chairman. Today the Pepkor Group consists of seven wholly owned subsidiaries that together operate more than 3 100 retail outlets in Africa, Australia and Poland, and employ more than 30 000 people. Christo is still chairman of Pepkor, as well as of Shoprite and Invicta, and serves as a non-executive director of Brait SA.

Despite his very tight schedule around the time we wanted to do the interview, Christo went out of his way to accommodate us. Everything had already been set up when he arrived strictly on time and indicated that we could start immediately. He was well prepared and, as was to be expected from a seasoned legal man, answered the questions in a relaxed and focused manner.

I started off with Christo's decision to join Renier van Rooyen's Pep Stores in 1967, after completing his legal studies. To put it into perspective: Pep Stores was founded in 1965 with a single store in Upington in the northern Cape. By 1970, the group had grown to 114 stores. What was it like to be part of such a young and dynamic group? Christo describes it as 'an exciting time', especially on account of the people he worked with. He admits, however, that the retail sector was 'a bit off the mark' of the profession for which his university studies had trained him, to his father's dismay.

Renier van Rooyen, the founder of Pep Stores, strongly believed that senior personnel had to be shareholders in the business. When I ask Christo about this principle, he explains that, when Renier started expanding his business, he was approached by various people who wanted to join him as employees and/or shareholders. His 'rule' that he put to them was simple: 'You can't occupy a position as store manager if you're not a shareholder, and you can't become a shareholder unless you work for the company.'

After seven years at Pep Stores, Christo resigned as executive director to practise as an advocate at the Cape Bar. He highlights three factors that motivated his decision to practise law, 'which I enjoyed very much'. The first had to do with his role within Pep Stores. After the company listed on the JSE in 1972, it naturally 'lost some of its character of a family business'. As founder, managing director and chairman, Renier was 'the number-one man in the business. I was the number-two man and I wouldn't have had it any other way, but I didn't really see myself as someone who would want to occupy the number-two role in the long term.' A second consideration was his academic background in law, a field 'to which I was strongly attuned', and he was attracted by what 'I suppose one can call the romanticism of a legal practice'. Many of his friends were at the Bar. Thirdly, he had started thinking about marriage, and 'with the way we worked in Pep Stores in those years it wouldn't have been a very good beginning for a marriage, because I was away from home 20 days a month'.

In 1981, however, Christo returned to Pep Stores. What had changed in the meantime, he explains, was that Renier had decided that he wanted to retire 'and he and I started talking'. At that stage, 'my shareholding was already the same as his, and we agreed that I would buy him buy out and then return to the business as the majority shareholder and executive chairman.'

In 1982 the name of the holding company was changed to Pepkor. Today the group is not only one of South Africa's business giants, but also trades successfully in other African countries, and in Australia and Poland. In reply to my question about milestones in Pepkor's success story, Christo says immediately that there were 'lots of highlights and of course also a good dose of lows'. For him, the major highlights were, firstly, 'to see how much growth potential there was in the business, because the model was right, aimed at the right segment of the market with the right kind of business philosophy; and, secondly, being able to witness, over the decades, how many people had grown within the business, achieved success and become much bigger people than they had ever imagined they could be. That goes for me too. The business became much bigger than I could ever have envisaged in those first years.'

Over the years, Christo has received many accolades, including an honorary doctorate. It would be hard for him 'to single out any of those acknowledgements as the outstanding highlight', he says, 'because in the course of your life you also get quite a few slaps in the face, and you're just grateful for anything that looks like some measure of recognition'. He has always accepted 'that whatever recognition I receive is actually given to me as the representative of a group of people, because that which was accomplished was not done by me alone. Thousands of people have contributed to the success that the group became.'

On the topic of success, Christo likes to refer to the saying that 'you can accomplish anything if you don't care who gets the credit'. What he means by this is that achievements such as Pepkor's are always collaborative efforts. 'It's about hundreds or thousands of people, or, in our case, tens of thousands, working together who should actually get the credit for what has been accomplished. If you always want to hog the limelight and insist that *you* did it, you're not telling the truth, firstly, and, secondly, it cannot serve as motivation for the people who have walked that road with you.'

In one of the group's annual reports, Christo makes the rather surprising statement that the biggest competition comes from individual businesses, not from large companies. 'Pep Stores is an excellent example of this,' he explains. When Pep Stores was founded, 'the retail scene in South Africa was totally dominated by OK Bazaars and Greatermans – the owners of Stuttafords and later also the owners of Checkers. And that small store that started in Upington ultimately took over both those businesses.'

Christo has a reputation for not being scared to take big decisions that are, in many cases, considered risky. In his view, risk is part of an entrepreneur's life. 'I often tell people that to be a successful entrepreneur you really need to be a bit crazy. If every morning when you get up you think of all the disasters that may strike you that day, most of which are totally outside of your control, but you still risk everything you have in order to realise your ideal – is that not a bit insane? Many people who've had a business career of about 30 to 40 years will tell you that if they knew at the outset how hard it would be they would never have taken that road. That's one side of the coin.

The other side is that, when you look back, it actually seems as if it was so easy.'

When you talk to Christo, you soon realise that he is very positive about South Africa and Africa, so much so that he detests Afropessimists and lets fly at them at times. In the first place, he says, 'I'm by nature a positive kind of person. I've never been able to fathom what benefit one derives from being negative. As we know, there are two sides to the world and to life.' Moreover, his family has been in South Africa for more than 350 years. 'What else am I really except an African and a South African? How can I become negative about my environment, my country and my people?' But besides what he calls the 'emotional side', Christo also believes that 'there is enough evidence today, when one looks objectively at South Africa and Africa, that this continent's time has come. The macro figures prove it; a year or so ago, six or seven African countries were among the world's ten fastest-growing economies.'

In his view, why are South Africans often so negative about the country? According to Christo, over the years South Africans, and white South Africans in particular, have become accustomed to the notion that 'Pretoria will fix everything'. He believes that the previously advantaged group has a responsibility to demonstrate to those who were previously disadvantaged that people can and should do something for themselves. 'Unfortunately, in many cases that example is just not being set, because the moaning never stops. "The municipality has not fixed the pothole in the street in front of my house" – and then the people live in a house worth millions of rand and it costs R50 to fix the hole, but they won't do it themselves. They're waiting for the municipality to do it. What example are we setting to people living in areas where they don't even have tarred roads?'

Christo has been involved in various industries, but, regardless of the nature of a particular business, he believes that people are invariably the decisive success factor. 'It all boils down to the quality of the management. That guy who simply goes the extra mile, gets up an hour earlier, stays up an extra hour to complete a task – it's people's passion that makes everything. Nothing else.'

When it comes to advice to young people who may be contemplating emigration, Christo says that, in recent years, it 'has become increasingly easier for me to say: "Just look around you here and then take a look at the rest of the world" – the old saying of the grass always being greener on the other side of the fence. Look at what has been happening in Europe. One economist after the other tells you there's no chance that Europe will recover in the next five to ten years. Most countries in the eurozone are bankrupt.' Among a 'whole list of drawbacks', he cites Europe's ageing population, the lack of natural resources and growing competition from other parts of the world. 'Would you rather be there, where your pension and everything else are under threat, than here?'

Apart from the economic possibilities, he believes that 'we are living in paradise' when one considers the climate, the food we eat and our relatively small population. One thing that always strikes him in Europe, he says, is that 'regardless of how wealthy you may be, you're always among thousands of people when you pass through an airport, walk down a street or drive in traffic. We are free here. When we, particularly in the Cape, are caught in a traffic jam for ten minutes, we're extremely upset. People in London sit in traffic jams for an hour, an hour and a half.'

After the interview was broadcast, Sake24 requested permission to publish it in the form of an article in *Beeld*, *Die Burger* and *Volksblad*. This was not a compliment for me, but an indication of the respect they have for Christo and also of how refreshing it is to hear the views of someone who is in essence a proud South African.

CORE ELEMENTS FOR BUSINESS SUCCESS

According to Christo, at Pep Stores they believed that, just as every individual should have a philosophy of life, every business should have a philosophy. Renier van Rooyen, the founder of the group, captured theirs in five principles:

- Belief
- Hard work
- Enthusiasm
- Positive thinking
- Compassion for people.

'When you have those five elements in your business and build on them, it *has* to be a success.'

CHAPTER 26

Charl Senekal

FARMER AND OWNER OF SENEKAL SUGAR
Interview broadcast on 15 July 2012

Charl's father was a teacher. After 13 years as a laboratory technician in the sugar industry, Charl decided to acquire a small farm and take on the gamble of becoming a sugar-cane farmer. From these modest beginnings, Charl has built up his farming business into one of the biggest private sugar producers in the world.

wanted to include one of South Africa's bigger and more successful farmers among the guests on the programme. A farmer is essentially a businessperson and is usually an entrepreneur *par excellence*. The only difference between a farmer and other business leaders is that he or she specialises in primary food production.

One name cropped up repeatedly in my inquiries – the sugar farmer Charl Senekal. Charl was named South Africa's Farmer of the Year in 2003. He is actively involved in the development of emerging farmers, and believes that farmers have a responsibility to help uplift their surrounding communities. We travelled to Mkuze in northern KwaZulu-Natal to talk to Charl on his game farm just outside the town.

Charl grew up with the message that the Senekals have to work for other people, not for themselves. Did this mindset affect his self-confidence when he embarked on a business of his own? Charl admits promptly that he never doubted his abilities. 'What I did doubt, was whether I would ever get the opportunity to prove myself. And it took very hard work to get there.'

After 13 years as a laboratory technician in the sugar industry, he decided to go into farming. He acquired a small farm of 45ha and resigned from his job. When I ask Charl whether he ever doubted the wisdom of this decision to swap a position in the formal sector for the uncertainty and risks of agriculture, he replies firmly: 'Not once.' After farming for about a month, he did return temporarily to his old workplace for six weeks as a stand-in for his former boss: 'the money he paid me came in quite handy, as I had to pay the transfer costs on my farm.' Charl's wife was left in charge of the farm during his absence, 'and I have to say that her farming was every bit as good as mine'.

I wanted to find out from Charl whether the experience he had gained as a sugar technician in the industry contributed to his subsequent success. Would he recommend to young people that they first work in a particular industry before launching their own business? In his own case, Charl believes, it was 'absolutely the right thing to have done. I acquired an enormous amount of experience in the factory itself; I was also the chief analytical chemist of the sugar mill and head of the cane-testing division, and I had the time to refine my skills. I was a polished diamond by the time I started farming.' He did 'every possible course that was presented by the sugar industry', and these were free of charge to boot. 'The day I began on the farm, I knew more about sugar farming than most extension officers do.'

From that first little farm, Charl has progressed to being one of the biggest private sugar farmers in the world, with a diesel bill of up to R200 000 per day and a monthly electricity bill in excess of R1.2 million. To what does he attribute this success? 'Total commitment,' he says immediately. 'My whole family helped me to accomplish it. It's a beautiful story to tell, but there were days that we struggled. Yet the determination, the courage and the perseverance just stayed with me and today, after 32 years in the industry as a farmer, I'm still as enthusiastic about the farming business as I was the day that I started it.'

A major turning point in the Senekal farming operations was the building of the Jozini pipeline, which supplies Mkuze with water from the Jozini Dam (previously the Pongolapoort Dam). The story behind this pipeline provides a clear example of Charl's resoluteness and innovative thinking. A project that would have cost more than R40 million ten years ago, and that was considered impossible to execute, was implemented successfully by Charl at about half the price. I wanted to hear from Charl himself how this came about. They naturally followed the correct channels in their attempt to obtain approval for the project, he says, and 'it went quite smoothly at first. Everyone said that it was needed, but we kept waiting for the permission to be given.'

On 31 December 1999, Charl listened in his flat in Durban to then deputy president Jacob Zuma's New Year's message in which he declared that 2000 would be 'the year of basic services to the people'. Early in January 2000 Charl contacted Zuma in Cape Town and told him: 'We've heard what you said, and we like it a lot. We live in Mkuze – he knows Mkuze very well. We want to lay a water pipeline, but we hear that the state wants to do it. Please, don't let the state do it; I will do it. I'll provide water to the same community that you want to service with the state money, which amounted to more than R210 million.'

When Zuma asked him what the catch was, Charl said that he wanted water from the Jozini Dam for his sugar plantations. Zuma was very enthusiastic about the project and wanted Charl and his wife to travel to Cape Town without delay so that he could listen to their story. 'The following day we were packing our cases when the phone rang and Mr Zuma's secretary told us to sit tight, the deputy president was coming to us. Two days later he arrived, and we had a wonderful conversation.' Zuma was 'highly impressed with the project' and said that they could proceed with it, but it had to be completed within a year. So Charl put his problem to Zuma; he was ready to start, 'but I still have to comply with this long list of about 30 points before I'm past Environmental Affairs and the rest. Then he said to me, "Don't you get it? I have just given you the go-ahead."'

According to Charl, the pipeline 'was one of the things that established the Senekal farming operations. It was that something that you do that no one else was prepared to tackle.' The day they bought the farm from Anglo American and signed the contracts in Pietermaritzburg, Charl says, 'the man told me, "Oh, you're obviously thinking that you will get water from the dam?" I have to admit that he had read my thoughts, but he said that Anglo American couldn't pull it off, and Charl Senekal definitely wouldn't pull it off. And today that farm supplies water to 350 000 people.'

I wanted to bring our conversation back to the commercial farmers and their role in the country. Charl's enthusiasm is infectious as he elaborates on their leadership role and why he is so proud of being a farmer in South Africa. In South Africa, he says, 'a farmer is a leader and he is recognised as such'. Charl reckons that about 99% of 'the big commercial farmers, the super-farmers, are already involved in community upliftment – building schools, providing bus services, providing water, giving agricultural advice'.

They have agreed with the government that they will expand this involvement, 'because a commercial farmer in our country is a walking library of farming knowledge. I always say that it's farming knowledge in action. People know that you can throw any situation on the table for them, and they will come up immediately with a very good solution.' To Charl, it is crucially important that this expertise be transferred 'to the small farmer in order to make him a big farmer too'. As he puts it, 'I would like them to be able to thrive. I don't want them to take my farm. I want to help them turn their farm into one like mine. That makes sense, doesn't it? Then we would have two farms that can produce in this country, because, at this stage, I believe everyone is already aware of the fact that the world will be facing a food crisis from about 2025, and we need to be prepared for that time.'

Given the political uncertainty in South Africa, would Charl still have opted to become a farmer if he had to make that choice today? There is clearly no doubt in his mind. 'For sure,' he says with conviction. 'It's my calling. It's what I love to do.' Because he is 'something of a people person', he enjoys 'turning an enemy into a friend, and you do that very easily by selling him a better bottom line'.

I asked Charl about his support base in managing one of the world's biggest sugar producers. When he looks back, what have they done right? Charl reckons that over the past 25 years he appointed excellent people, 'experts in our industry who support me enormously'. But his strongest support comes from his three sons, Dreyer, Charl and André. 'Nothing is too big for us to tackle', and they are the ones who encourage him to embark on new projects. As an example, Charl mentions their agreement with a Belgian firm specialising in renewable energy to establish a power plant to generate 'green' electricity on the farm. At the same time, the Senekals are involved in a big expansion of their sugar-farming operations. These are massive projects and 'many people would be scared to undertake them simultaneously, but we do them at the same time because I delegate'. His daughter got married recently, Charl adds, 'and she has brought another good farmer to the party'.

In the course of the interview I was struck by the almost shy way in which Charl believes in himself and his abilities. It testifies to an inherent humility, coupled with an unshakeable faith in what he does. When I ask him what he means by saying that you should trust in yourself, he explains: 'Believe that no one can do it better than you can. Pray. Ask the Lord, "Give me strength. Give me insight. Help me to solve this problem." And once you've done that, you still need to believe in yourself. You have to say, "I'm not an ordinary person. I want to be an extraordinary person." Share your knowledge, your experience and your happiness with others, because in that way you advance.'

When I reflected on the interview, I realised once again what an important role a successful business, in this case a farming business, plays in the community, and how one tends to skim too quickly over this fact. At the same time, successful commercial farmers have a responsibility to uplift the communities in and around their farming operations; after my conversation with Charl, I am convinced that the vast majority of these farmers are tackling this enormous task with pride.

KEY ADVICE TO A YOUNG FARMER

- Farmers can fail to give enough attention to the financial affairs of the farming operation. 'When you start on a farm, you have to know that you can meet your obligations this month, and that you can meet them the following month.' He adds that you should draw up a budget immediately, and 'control it with an iron hand'.

- Be determined and don't lose courage.
- Do as much of the work as is possible yourself.
- Be disciplined. 'Once they get an income, many guys immediately buy a 4x4 and the wife gets a small car, and then they start running into cash-flow problems. The bank only laughs at such undisciplined guys, but for the guy who is disciplined, they have lots of time and lots of money.'

ADVICE TO YOUNG PEOPLE WHO WANT TO START THEIR OWN BUSINESS

- Do your homework thoroughly.
- Discuss your plan with experts and listen to their advice.
- Make sure that your financial affairs are in order.
- Believe in yourself and trust in yourself.

CHAPTER 27

Dr Chris van der Merwe

FOUNDER AND CHIEF EXECUTIVE OF THE PRIVATE EDUCATION GROUP CURRO HOLDINGS | *Interview broadcast on 22 July 2012*

Chris and his sister were brought up by their mother after their father died at an early age. The family struggled financially, but this did not deter Chris from pursuing his dreams. He qualified as a primary school teacher and taught for a number of years. In 1997 he obtained his doctorate from Stellenbosch University with a thesis that focused on excellence in schools. He started Curro in 1998 with a single school and a big overdraft. Today the Curro Group is a JSE-listed company with a market value of more than R3 billion.

Before, during and after the interview, one aspect stood out as plain as day: Chris's whole life revolves around the education of children, how it can be done and how it can be improved. When Chris showed me around Curro's head office before we started our formal interview, two things in particular caught my attention. The first was the stack of applications from parents wanting to enrol their children at the various Curro schools in the coming years. It seemed a great pity that the number of applications far exceeded the available places. The second striking element was the use of technology; Chris knows exactly how every child in every grade in every school is performing, and, likewise, how every teacher's pupils are performing, down to the level of a progress test!

Our conversation began with Chris's childhood in a single-parent household (he was just three years old when his father died). Chris pays tribute to his mother, who brought him and his sister up 'with great dedication' and ensured that they developed well 'through her positive thinking and her firm belief in good education'. What he will never forget is that she 'instilled in us that we could rise above our circumstances', and made them believe in themselves.

Early in the interview, the teacher in Chris emerges, with advice about when to send your child to school. Chris himself went to school a year too early, 'and always felt that emotionally I wasn't quite at the same level as my classmates'. In the teaching profession, 'we have found without a doubt that it's very good to hold the child back' at an early enough stage if he or she is emotionally behind. He stresses, however, that this should happen early, 'I would say at about grade R/grade 1'.

After school, Chris decided to become a primary school teacher. While the decision worked out very well for him and teaching was his passion, his financial position meant that he did not really have any other choice. 'Our principal called all the grade 11 boys one day and simply stated that there was a lack of male teachers at primary school level: "The Education Department is making bursaries available:

173

who wants to make use of this opportunity?" And, from a logical perspective, many of us grasped it.'

Before moving on to his career, first as teacher and later as businessman, I wanted to get Chris's views on the role that his postgraduate studies played in his development and subsequent success. In Chris's opinion, a strong academic background gives one 'a great deal of confidence'. When entrepreneurs ask him what the golden rule is, he remarks, 'I always reply spontaneously: "You have to be a master of the product or the service that you want to offer."' He believes that his doctoral study on excellence in schools helped him to 'gain a full understanding of the kind of service that would work in the context of South African education'.

In 1993 Chris took his first steps in the business world with a business plan for Skoolkor, which was aimed at producing material to help schools with their curricula. According to Chris, they were six teachers without any business experience when they started the enterprise. The bank helped them to draw up 'a mini business plan' in terms of which they had to borrow R60 000. Each partner had to stand surety for R10 000. Chris recalls that when he told his mother about this, she just remarked: 'Son, dangerous business.' The venture worked quite well, he says, although the challenge was 'to keep the expenditure below that overdraft limit at all times'. He reckons that this helped him to develop his business skills over the years.

Chris highlights two lessons from the Skoolkor experience. Firstly, it was almost a shock to discover 'what an enormous turnover in rand value had to be generated for a small net profit'. The second lesson he learnt was that 'when you market your product with passion and believe in it, you get a lot of clients to support you. Not forgetting, of course, that it has to be a good product.'

At a personal level, Skoolkor made a greater contribution to the development of Chris van der Merwe than could be measured in money. According to Chris, 'it planted the seed in me of the idea that

I could generate my own income through my own efforts, which was quite good for my self-image. In fact, I think Skoolkor prepared me in terms of developing enough business acumen with which we could start running Curro schools.'

Curro was started in 1998, in the vestry of the Bergsig Dutch Reformed church in Durbanville. What led to this step? Chris explains that he was deputy principal of the Fanie Theron Primary School in Kraaifontein when he obtained his doctorate in 1997 and applied for a position as curriculum expert at the Department of Education. When he didn't get the job, he and his wife concluded, after an in-depth discussion, that there was a market for 'a small, niche private school, so we took the decision and started a school'. The state had indicated at the time that it intended scrapping the Model C system. Given their teaching background, Chris and his wife knew 'how good this product actually was, and our reasoning was that we would merely be giving the product back to the community, but at a cost'.

As in the case of many new businesses, it was one thing to have a business plan and an opportunity; the real test lay in the execution of the plan, and for that they needed capital. In May 1999 Chris calculated that they required R1 million to implement their plan. He had some experience of building houses, which stood him in good stead once they had started Curro and realised that they would have to build a campus. 'I put up my hand and offered to build the school, drew up a very simple business plan and approached Absa for the R7 million we needed.' He believes that the bank approved it because it was 'a clean and honest' model that met a need. Parents preferred smaller classes to the big classes in public schools and there was uncertainty around state education, 'since no one knew what the implications of outcomes-based education would be for the country'.

The next big step in the growth of Curro came in 2009 with the acquisition of a stake in the business by the PSG Group, followed by the highly successful listing on the JSE. This would propel Curro into the big league, but, as Chris recounts, there was nevertheless a bit of luck involved in the creation of 'the marriage' between them and PSG. The parents of the Hazeldene Primary School in Pretoria East wanted to have a separate high school, while Curro's model at the time was 'to give the community a combined school where all the children – from grade R to grade 12 – are taught on one campus'. At a conference, one of the parents, Jan van Wyk, asked Jannie Mouton of PSG if he wanted to become involved in that high school. 'Two weeks later, Jannie came to see us and asked if he could invest 50% in the whole Curro Group,' says Chris. 'So he invested R50 million in a business of which the market capitalisation was determined to be R100 million in 2009. That started the marriage between us and PSG, and we designed a new business plan that set our goal at 40 schools by 2020.'

Today Curro has a market value of more than R3 billion, and that from a business plan drawn up by an educationist with a passion for pedagogy. It was easy to conclude from the interview that Chris knows exactly what he is doing when it comes to education, but I was interested in finding out what he considers the most important elements as far as financing and cash flow are concerned. Chris believes that, as an entrepreneur, you have to 'put all your cards on the table' and be totally honest with your banker. His understanding of your business model should be as good as your own. 'If you don't share everything, both positive and negative, with your banker, he won't be able to understand your business fully and I reckon he won't be so willing to walk an aggressive road with you.'

His 'red book' served as his 'compass', Chris explains. 'Any business needs a compass, because every day you as an entrepreneur have to evaluate your business and yourself in order to determine whether the boat is still sailing in the right direction.' When his wife still did the books of the business, they used to calculate the annual turnover, divide it by 12 months and then divide the monthly turnover by 30 days. Every morning at nine o'clock she would draw a bank statement of their account's balance. Chris says that his red book 'predicted the daily balance including the income and expenditure'; if the result he received at nine in the morning tallied with the prediction, 'I knew that the business was going in the right direction'.

After the interview, I was swamped with inquiries, especially from parents and teachers. The golden thread that ran through the questions was simple: parents wanted to know whether Chris was going to open a school in their region, and teachers wanted to know where they could send their CVs. This enthusiastic response on the part of viewers also provided the best encapsulation of my own impressions.

ADVICE TO ENTREPRENEURS ON HOW TO TURN A BUSINESS PLAN INTO A SUCCESSFUL BUSINESS

- You should be a master of your product or service. This gives you a competitive advantage as well as 'the confidence to market your product with passion and belief'.
- You have to put in the necessary hours and should realise that it will require a lot of dedication.
- Your calculations and expectations should be realistic, and you need to monitor your cash-flow streams on a daily basis.
- You should realise that you will be faced with enormous challenges, maybe even bankruptcy. 'Life consists of a concept of ebb and flow' and you will have to contend with this 'during your entire career – sometimes good times, sometimes bad times'.
- Never lose courage, even when the tide turns against you. 'If you've become completely disheartened, just try one more time.'
- Get the support of your family, especially your spouse. Put them in the picture and share your business plan with them so that 'they can tackle every opportunity or challenge with you, because this gives you the ability to absorb the pressure with much greater ease'.

CHAPTER 28

Peter Scott

OWNER AND CHIEF EXECUTIVE OF MR. VIDEO
Interview broadcast on 29 July 2012

Peter grew up in a home where his father had a bicycle shop and his mother a furniture store. As a schoolboy, he did part-time work to earn pocket money, first at a cinema and then, from the age of 15, at a video rental store. Movies are his passion, and he started his own video rental chain as a 19-year-old. Four years later, Peter sold this business, and in 1994 he founded Mr. VIDEO. The group currently consists of more than 200 franchise outlets across South Africa and in Namibia – the largest movie rental business in Africa. Peter is also involved in the financing and production of films in South Africa.

Peter's story, in a nutshell, is that of the guy who started working in a video rental store as a schoolboy and ended up as the owner of the largest movie rental business in the country. What stood out most clearly during our conversation was his passion for movies and everything related to them.

We shot the interview in a cinema at his house. If you look at the memorabilia and give Peter an opportunity, he will tell you about his encounters with just about every superstar in the movie world, with photographs to add colour. This total passion was the driving force behind the success of the boy in the video rental store who advanced to become the owner of the Mr. VIDEO Group and financial backer of some of South Africa's best-known feature films.

Owing to a lack of pocket money, Peter started working in a cinema as a schoolboy so that he could watch movies. But the problem with being a cinema employee, he explains, is that you 'never got to watch the beginning and the end of movies' on account of your tasks. At the age of 15, he swapped this part-time job for one in a video rental store. They were supposed to close the doors at eight in the evening, but, as a result of Peter's craving to watch movies from beginning to end, he kept the store open until ten o'clock. The store did extra business, the customers were delighted, and the owner was so impressed with the higher turnover that 'he just wanted me to do more and more shifts. So eventually I worked as many shifts as possible.' It was no wonder that the customers gave Peter the nickname 'Mr Video'.

Peter had finished school by the time the owner decided to sell the video store. Many people would have viewed this as a setback, but, in Peter's case, he saw it as an opportunity. He approached the owner and pleaded for a chance to buy the business: 'I really love what I do and I would like to start my own business, please help me.' With the R500 he had to his name Peter built shelves, which he painted blue with paint he got from his father. The owner sold him the movies as well: 'I could pay the money off over six months, and that's how I started my first business.'

As is the case with any entrepreneur, the initial months were tough. Peter recounts wryly that the business was burgled on the very first evening that they opened – there was no money for an alarm system. Their entire evening's turnover, 'my first R150 that I made', was gone.

Over the next few years, he expanded the business and added more stores. But when he was in his mid-twenties, he sold his video store group after someone had made him an offer. When he looks back on this decision, however, Peter says that he realises the deal was a mistake and that he was blinded by the purchase price. 'Sometimes you have to think twice before you sell,' he admits. 'Sometimes you need to hold on to what you have and not let go too soon.'

After selling his business Peter spent four years in Knysna, which he describes as 'actually a good period'. As he puts it, 'I sat down a bit, thought a bit, and planned my future'. This was where the concept of the Mr. VIDEO Group was devised. He had the opportunity to reflect on all the aspects of his envisaged business, not only what he wanted to do differently but also what the name should be. After struggling for a while to find an appropriate name, he says, 'it suddenly popped into my head one day: Mr. VIDEO'.

Mr. VIDEO was launched in 1994 and the group has since grown to more than 200 stores. To what does he ascribe the group's success? Peter puts his 'enormous passion for the business' at the top of his list, followed by perseverance and hard work. The most important elements, he believes 'were the many hours of work and the passion that I have,' combined with good service to his customers.

In response to my question about his views on the future of the movie rental industry, Peter speaks frankly about the stumbling blocks they face. To deal with the challenge of changing technology, he says, they have to innovate and do things better 'in order to stay ahead of the technology'. According to him, South Africa is still far behind the rest of the world in this regard, which benefits their industry. Their biggest problem, he maintains, is piracy and the fact that the laws that prohibit it are not enforced. In his view, legislation that prevents the group from buying movies independently overseas and bringing them into the country is another major stumbling block that could lead to job losses.

Peter has a very specific philosophy about opportunities. He believes that all people get opportunities; the difference lies in what they do with them. 'Some people get an opportunity and simply let it go by,' he explains. 'Some get an opportunity but they don't use it fully, while others make a success of the opportunity they get.' Peter refers to a saying of his father's that 'every person gets five golden years', and says that he believes his five golden years still lie ahead.

The core of this interview was the principle of passion: passion for the industry. In Peter's case, what he does for a living is not a job – it's a way of life. If you ever want a shining example of someone whose entertainment or hobby also happens to be his work, you don't have to look further than Peter.

ADVICE TO YOUNG ENTREPRENEURS

- 'If you're not going to be passionate about what you do, rather don't do it.'
- Perseverance is vital. He illustrates this point with a quotation: 'The secret of success is hanging on after others have let go.'
- You must be actively involved in your business; this is where the passion and the principle of perseverance come together.

WHAT QUALITIES DO FRANCHISEES NEED TO BE SUCCESSFUL IN A FRANCHISE BUSINESS (WHETHER IT BE A RESTAURANT OR A MOVIE RENTAL STORE)?

- The franchisee should be an 'operator' with passion, not an investor.
- They should be involved in the day-to-day management of the business. Some people 'only want to come by once a week to pick up the money; that doesn't work'.

CHAPTER 29

Dr André Fourie

CHIEF EXECUTIVE OF POYNTING ANTENNAS

Interview broadcast on 5 August 2012

André grew up in an Afrikaans environment in towns such as Welkom and Klerksdorp. In 1981 he decided to study Engineering at the University of the Witwatersrand (Wits). He obtained his doctorate in 1991 and became one of the youngest science professors at Wits in 1992. André and a few colleagues started Poynting Antennas in 2001, and in 2005 he resigned from academia to join Poynting on a full-time basis. Poynting was listed on the JSE in 2008. Today the group has over 120 employees and a turnover in excess of R80 million.

I have come to know André as a self-effacing person with a razor-sharp mind. You don't engage in a debate with him without making sure that you have marshalled your facts and arguments. There are people who are academically clever and others who are well read; when someone has both of these attributes, you have to know what you're talking about!

Our conversation started with André's decision to tackle an Engineering course in English at Wits despite his very Afrikaans home and school background. The adjustment to the unfamiliar environment of Wits was hard at first, André admits. 'I always say that the only contact I had with English-speaking people while growing up in towns like Welkom and Krugersdorp was when we had gangs as boys; we would throw stones and swear at each other in our respective languages.' But he was adventurous and wanted to experience a different culture. His respect for Wits as an academic institution also played a part in his decision, 'although at that stage they were considered politically undesirable' in the environment from which he hailed. The adjustment difficulties in his first year were exacerbated by the fact that he came from a public school background – many of his fellow students had attended private schools. While he was 'way behind' at first, it became easier over time.

Once he had acclimatised, André thrived in academia; he obtained his doctorate in 1991 and was appointed a professor at a very young age. But his response is rather unexpected when I ask about his views on the value of a strong academic background for business success. As a businessman, he doesn't consider it such a good idea; 'our heroes like Steve Jobs and Bill Gates', who devoted their time to starting and running their businesses instead of completing their university degrees, 'are in fact the better entrepreneurs'.

In his own case, André says, he was quite 'passionate' about his discipline as an academic. He liked academia, 'devising new things and working on them in cooperation with academic people'. He describes the atmosphere within which he worked at the university as 'fantastic, because, in those days, Wits allowed you to do whatever you wanted to'. You could start your own business, which he and some colleagues did at the time. André reckons that the situation that obtained there was 'actually what made it possible for me because, given my background, I was not really the type of person that would become an entrepreneur. But that was where I decided that I wanted to start my own thing.'

What has stayed in his mind when he thinks back to his days at Wits is the freedom they were given as academics. You could take on private work if you wanted to and when it took up more than 20% of your time they paid you a bit less, but you could continue with your work as lecturer as long as you delivered what the university required from you: good students, postgraduate candidates and articles published in academic journals. 'This is important for a university, and I believe that it was a fantastically empowering situation. Companies like Internet Solutions came out of Wits, and in my view it's due to the fact that they allowed that freedom.'

In 2001 André started Poynting Antennas together with eight other 'techies' at Wits. Most of them had started out as students of his, but some had obtained MSc degrees and doctorates in the meantime. How did this business work, and why was it started at that particular point? As André explains it, by that time they had been running a consulting business at Wits for almost ten years, doing work that often included 'highly advanced military work for aircraft and ships and that type of thing'. This consulting work frequently also drove their research interests, but he says he kept feeling that 'a real businessman' is not someone who runs a consulting business. 'I think we all felt we could do something big in this world, so we decided in 2000 to start manufacturing antennas because that was a real business, not a play-play business any more.' They acquired a huge building in the Johannesburg suburb of Wynberg, where properties were 'dirt cheap' at the time. The nine colleagues moved into three offices in the building, 'and from there the company expanded'.

Today, Poynting is a business with a 120-strong workforce that includes many highly qualified scientists. Why would an extremely competent team, with specialised skills, decide to focus on antennas specifically in South Africa?

André ascribes the attractiveness of the idea to the combination of high-tech design skills and low-tech manufacturing. While the design work is highly complicated and specialised, the manufacturing process is relatively simple. 'In a South African context, you need relatively low-tech manufacturing – in other words, people who can screw things together. These are simple processes that are available, and I believe it's ideal for South Africa.'

I wanted us to look more closely at the issue of technology and how one transforms a brilliant idea into a successful business. This former professor has managed to do just that; the business has been listed successfully on the JSE, and their products are exported worldwide. What does he recommend to innovators who believe that they have promising idea?

André reckons that he is well placed to give sound advice, by virtue of his own experience and the lessons he and his colleagues have learnt. Companies like theirs, he says, 'usually start with technical guys'. While technology-minded people have the ability to come up with smart ideas, they tend to have 'an excessive belief' in their products. 'We play with our own toys instead of looking at the market, and I believe the most important aspect is the market and marketing.' They don't invest in people who can market their product and neglect to do thorough market research. 'So one of the first things to keep in mind is that you need to do proper marketing. You have to know that there are people who are physically going to take money from their pocket and buy your product, that there are enough of them out there, and that you have the people who are going to persuade the customers to make the purchase. If you don't have that, you're on a very, very dangerous path.'

On the initial steps in turning an innovative idea into a business, André adds that raising start-up capital will always be your first problem. 'Don't get capital from venture capitalists,' he warns, because they will put you in a very difficult position. 'Rather start small and ensure that you can make enough money to get the business going on your own steam. Place your product in a little niche where it can at least start selling to some extent.' He advises that you have to make sure that 'you can start making money and are able to show what you can do before you even contemplate the idea of getting money from anyone else'. He also highlights the importance of getting financial people involved in the business at an early stage.

According to André, the listing of Poynting Antennas on the JSE in 2008 was prompted by their dreams of becoming a world leader in their field. To realise this, the company wants to be in a position to acquire other companies that fit in with their business, and for this they need the investments and capital to which the listing gives them access. The listing was a milestone that signalled their intentions for the future, not only to themselves but also to the outside world.

I asked André what he means by insisting that people in a working situation ought to be motivated by the notion of 'making a difference'. He emphasises this as a core principle, whether in life or in business. If you want to start a business for the sole purpose of making money, he believes, you should rather focus only on investments or something of that nature. In the case of Poynting Antennas, they were motivated by the desire to make products that 'would enable people to communicate, to make connections'. André feels very strongly that one should be driven by an urge that says: 'I want to do something for humanity.' When you start working somewhere, he remarks, 'you should say: "I want to make a difference to this place"; we always say that the people who don't want to make a difference, don't matter.'

He refers to Gandhi's saying about 'being the difference you wish to see in the world', and confesses that he hates 'this complaining and whining about things' that is prevalent in South Africa. 'If there's a hole in the road and you haven't yet fixed two holes yourself, don't complain about holes in the road.' André believes passionately that 'if everyone had to make that small difference', we would have far fewer problems.

Throughout the interview, I detected a strong undertone of a very positive view of South Africa and Africa on André's part. Why does he single out this continent? 'To my mind, we're sitting in the most exciting place in the world,' he declares frankly. For a long time Africa has been viewed in a negative light because of the massive problems that followed after decolonisation, 'but of course this attitude is changing now that everyone realises Africa is the last big undeveloped part of the world'. He believes that the opportunities are fantastic: 'As they say, the buzz is here.' He has visited Europe as well as the countries to which South Africans tend to emigrate, such as Australia and the United States. 'Those places are dead compared to us,' André says. 'Here things are alive. People have opportunities. You can start something here with very little.'

PERSONAL BUSINESS ADVICE

In my opinion, gaining experience is difficult but important. Most people are in too much of a hurry to start a business when they are young and don't really want to do the experience part. I worked for a year for a small, one-man business that manufactured masts and antennas. I regard the experience I acquired there as extremely valuable even though the circumstances were tough. I was often at loggerheads with the relatively older owner of the business; owners of such one-man enterprises usually tend to be difficult and don't want anyone else to take decisions. After a year I gave the owner an ultimatum, saying that I wanted a majority stake in the antenna part of the business or else I would leave. I was fired on the spot! The next day I started my own business, but today I realise that what I learnt about cash flow, staff, sales, marketing, processes, etc was invaluable, regardless of the circumstances!

PRACTICALLY, AS A STARTING POINT

I would recommend that you search for a suitable small business where you would like to work, even if it is for a pittance. It needs to be a small enterprise so that you can come into contact with all aspects of a business (banking, customers, appointments, purchases, sales, etc). In addition, from the outset you should set yourself the goal of taking over the business, establishing a new subsidiary or resigning within two years, otherwise you will get too comfortable.

ON ACADEMIC QUALIFICATIONS

I believe that it's better not to do an MBA or a formal business course if you intend to become an entrepreneur. These qualifications are generally aimed at assuring you a massive salary in a large company, which tends to happen, and then it becomes hard to leave. It is also advantageous to start your own business at a young age, before you have too many family responsibilities. Marry someone who can also earn an income. So, business qualifications are not that important for a prospective entrepreneur. Read books, do short courses on topics such as financial management, sales and marketing. Form partnerships with specialists who are qualified in these fields, or appoint good people in your business.

CHAPTER 30

Beyers Truter

OWNER AND CHIEF EXECUTIVE OF BEYERSKLOOF WINE ESTATE
Interview broadcast on 12 August 2012

Beyers holds a BSc (Agric) degree from Stellenbosch University. With his mind set on winemaking, he obtained a position at Kanonkop, where he established himself as one of the country's leading winemakers and a Pinotage specialist. In 1988 he bought Beyerskloof, a wine estate that he has since put on the map as South Africa's foremost Pinotage brand.

When you meet Beyers, you are immediately struck by his passion for wine; it is in his blood and it is what he lives for, an integral part of his being. So it seemed apt to start our conversation with the culture of wine and where this passion originated.

Surprisingly, Beyers did not grow up with a culture of wine. His father was a hospital manager, and, at their home, the only manifestation of a wine culture was that 'my father had a glass of wine on Sundays and my mother perhaps an occasional tot of sweet wine'. His love for wine goes back to his high-school days at Jan van Riebeeck in Cape Town: 'I was about 14 years old when someone first introduced me to red wine, and I'm a guy who started collecting red wine while I was still at school.' Probably to his mother's regret, he adds, 'because I think mothers want their children to learn instead of making red-wine collecting their hobby'.

Beyers initially intended to study medicine, but in the end he graduated from Stellenbosch University with a BSc degree in Agriculture. On his way to qualifying as a vini- and viticulturalist, he was tripped up by Chemistry, to which he had to devote an extra year. The reason why he swapped his medical studies for winegrowing and winemaking, he says, is that 'after about six months of getting 80%, I realised that there were much better things to do at university. I should probably focus on my hobby, so I changed direction to study my hobby.' Of course there were other aspects of university life at Stellenbosch that were 'incredibly nice', such as rugby and social activities. 'Anyone who hasn't experienced that, hasn't yet experienced Stellenbosch.'

Since chemistry cropped up in our conversation, I wanted to know from Beyers why a sound knowledge of chemistry is indispensable for a winemaker. He observes jokingly that 'many young winemakers and other people believe it's some sort of cloud; the winemaker walks through the cloud and, lo and behold, the wine has been made'. That is not how it works, however: 'you have to know your chemistry'. When you pick up a glass of wine and smell and taste it, he says, 'you must also be able to see everything that's in it. When you read the chemical analysis, it has to give you an indication of the quality of the wine.'

When Beyers talks about his student years, he is as enthusiastic about his involvement in the Pieke Rugby Club as about his studies in the science of wine. He was the secretary of the club when they won all the cups in 1976. 'This is almost better than the World Cup for a student who didn't go further and just played a bit in the first league.' What he remembers most vividly from this time was 'the social part' – he was the member in charge of social activities on their residence committee, and they organised all kinds of activities with the women's residences. Beyers believes strongly that one gains valuable experience and organising skills by serving on such committees. 'I believe young people should never say "no" when they are nominated to do something in life or to serve on a committee.'

After completing his studies, Beyers started working at the Deciduous Fruit Board, but his mind was set on winemaking. Getting a position as winemaker, however, was no easy matter. How did he manage to get appointed at Kanonkop, one of the select wine estates? 'You won't believe me,' Beyers says, 'but it's one of those going-to-buy-bread-at-the-café stories.' When his wife sent him to the café one day to get a loaf of bread, he bumped into an acquaintance who told him that he had been offered the position of winemaker at Kanonkop but didn't consider himself ready for it. Beyers told him promptly: 'I'm not ready at all, but if the job is available, please ask the owners to contact me.' Oom Jannie Krige phoned him the following day and arranged to pick Beyers up 'at that same café' for an interview.

Luckily Professor Joel van Wyk's reference was supportive when Beyers's prospective employer contacted him to inquire about the applicant. As Beyers puts it, Van Wyk's recommendation was more or less as follows: 'This man likes rugby and a social life and he knows something about wine, so you can feel free to take a chance, I give it my stamp of approval.'

Before moving to Beyers's career as a winemaker, I wanted us to touch on the origins of Pinotage, the uniquely South African grape variety. Beyers explains that it was developed in 1925 by Professor Abraham Izak Perold in Stellenbosch as a cross between two French varieties, Pinot Noir and Cinsaut. (Cinsaut was known as Hermitage in South Africa at the time, hence the name 'Pinotage'.) 'There were four seedlings,' he says, 'and Pinotage was born from one of them.'

When I ask Beyers about his first years as a young winemaker at Kanonkop, he says that he had set his sights on Kanonkop when he was still a student – this was the place where he wanted to make wine. But once he found himself at the farm, 'I didn't even open the cellar doors in those first three or four weeks. I was too scared.' While his studies had equipped him for the 'technical part' of winemaking, he felt unprepared for the 'mechanical part'. When he overcame his fear and started making wine, the first trophy they won happened to be at a young wine show. 'In those days, the young wine show was everything' – if you won something there, 'you had made it.'

There is a story attached to the 1981 Cabernet Sauvignon that won them the trophy. According to Beyers, at the time the wine was being made, 'we worked from Tuesdays to Sundays without sleeping, and I had three or four workers in the cellar. Sometimes we had to push through up to 120 tons at a time – the workers caught naps on the cellar floor in between – and for that we would bring in a few extra people from the vineyard. One evening Kerneels, whom we called Soldaat, fell into the open vat and got out, leaving his shoes behind. And that year at the young wine show, the Cabernet Sauvignon from the vat containing Kerneels's shoes was named the best wine in Stellenbosch. So Kerneels, that loyal guy who would've done anything for me, was actually the one who put me on the path as winemaker.'

In the late 1980s, Beyers decided that he wanted to make his own wine on his own farm. When he saw the advertisement for a farm 'overlooking Simonsberg' that was for sale, he realised that 'this was the ideal spot'. The farm was in a state of neglect, 'with not a single vine that remained'. When Beyers looked at its history, he saw that wine had last been made there in 1955. 'That's the year in which I was born. So it all worked out, 100%.'

What does he regard as highlights in his career, particularly when it comes to his many wine awards? To Beyers, one award that stands out flowed from a wine-tasting event he hosted on the farm around 1982, where he was 'tremendously impressed' by a 1972 Simonsig Pinotage. Frans Malan from Simonsig was one of the icons in the industry; Beyers recounts that he plucked up his courage, phoned Malan and asked him how he made it. He had used new oak barrels, which was unheard of at the time. Beyers then started using new oak for Pinotage. 'And each time I ran a taste test, that wine that had been in the new wood barrels was finished long before the Pinotage that had matured in the usual way.' In those days there was resistance to wood, he says: 'People didn't want too much wood in wine.' His 1989 Pinotage was the first where he had added 30% new wood, and this wine contributed to the Robert Mondavi Trophy for the International Winemaker of the Year that Beyers won in 1991. 'It's probably the biggest award of all.' He reckons that 'it brought about quite a change in the industry', because he was the first South African to receive this trophy.

I was curious about the emphasis Beyers places on a period of ten years in the wine industry. It's all about ten years in a wine's lifetime, he explains in response to my question. Nowadays, vines are so well manipulated and the clones are so good that you can make good wine within five or six years, 'but old vines usually give you a much better tannin structure. When I make a wine, for example, I tend to allow myself ten years to experiment with all the possible variables until I achieve the best result, and after those ten years I usually say, give me another ten years.'

Beyers has made his name synonymous with a wine cultivar; Beyerskloof and Pinotage are inevitably linked in the world of wine, and he is commonly referred to as 'the king of Pinotage'. What did he do right to establish his name as a widely known brand? According to Beyers, Pinotage was 'something of a black sheep in the industry' when he started working with it, and they succeeded in raising the cultivar's reputation to a level where it enjoys not only national but also international recognition. While he always had a passion for wine, 'my passion for Pinotage was even stronger': as a tireless advocate for the wine, he conveyed the message 'by marketing it, by getting people to taste it, by speaking personally to them, and now I'm talking about many hours. It's no wonder that I've been losing my hair; it's on account of talking to people every day and making personal contact.' He reckons that the effort he has put into improving and championing the wine has led to his name being linked to Pinotage. At Beyerskloof, they not only make Pinotage but also Pinotage brandy, Pinotage port, and Pinotage rosé. In short, 'we are actually Pinotage-mad'.

Beyers Truter has succeeded in building a business around his own name as a brand, and, on top of that, has managed to link that name internationally to a particular wine cultivar. Dedicating yourself to one ten-year project after the other without knowing in advance whether your plans will work requires not only passion but an unyielding belief in what you do.

Pinotage owes a huge debt to Beyers Truter; without this indefatigable passion, which contributed to a change in the cultivar's fortunes, I suspect it might still be the black sheep of red wines today!

CHALLENGES WHEN BUILDING A BUSINESS AROUND YOUR OWN PERSON

- The most crucial aspect is personal contact 'and the extent to which you involve yourself with the customer. Making wine is easy, but marketing wine is one of the hardest jobs. You have to make personal contact without wasting the guy's time.'

- You must know your customers and make sure that in the end 'you even know what colour eyes the guy's wife has, how his dog barks. You must know everything about that guy.'
- Passion is everything. 'If a winemaker doesn't have passion, for his occupation, for his wife, for his animals, for his people, for the soil, he should stop and rather do something else.'

BEYERS'S OWN SUCCESS FACTORS

- 'Everything up to now has been achieved only by the grace of God. Some would say it was luck, but luck is also grace. And others would say I was in the right place at the right time, but that's grace too. Two major factors that play a role in the making of a good Pinotage are the soil and the climate – both God-given elements – once again, great grace.'
- 'Shoe leather. How many pairs of shoes did you wear out in order to tell your story and sell your wine? How many evenings did you have to forgo the pleasure of relaxing in front of the fire at home because you presented wine tastings? How many weeks were you on the road, locally and internationally, involved in food-and-wine evenings or interaction with customers to tell them about Pinotage and Beyerskloof? All of that is shoe leather.'
- 'Trail dust. The famous cowboy-philosopher Louis L'Amour said in one of his books: "Trail dust is thicker than blood." It was by no means a one-man show. It was a team effort in which all our farm workers, colleagues, winemakers, viticultural experts, the media and all Pinotage enthusiasts participated. I'm still covered in the dust of the trails I walked with all of them.'

- 'Last but not least, Pinotage is the only South African varietal that is available commercially in a bottle. It's unique: a USP (unique selling point) or, in my view, a HUSP – a huge unique selling point. That, of course, made it easy.'

CHAPTER 31

Braam van Huyssteen

FOUNDER AND CHIEF EXECUTIVE OF TEKKIE TOWN

Interview broadcast on 19 August 2012

Braam grew up in Parys in the Free State. He would do his homework in his mother's clothes shop in the afternoons, first in Parys and later in George after the family moved there when he was 12 years old. After obtaining a BEcon degree from Stellenbosch University, Braam opened his own store in Mossel Bay in 1989, with strong support from his entrepreneurial mother. In 1999 Braam did his first big transaction with a purchase of shoes to the value of R1.2 million, which led to him starting Tekkie Town with a single store in 2001. Over the next 12 years the group grew to 220 stores and a turnover of more than R1 billion. In 2011 Braam was named as the winner in the Master Entrepreneur category of the southern Africa chapter of the Ernst & Young World Entrepreneur Awards.

I contacted Braam via email to request an interview with him. As he was about to leave for London to attend the Olympic Games and we were in KwaZulu-Natal for other interviews, we decided to do the interview while he was coincidentally on a visit to Durban. The first thing that struck me was his orange jacket; he attributes his partiality for that colour to growing up in the Free State. And he makes no bones about the fact that he is a Cheetahs supporter to the marrow.

It was clear from the outset that Braam grew up in his mother's shop and that retail has always been part of his life. What role did his mother play in his career as an entrepreneur? According to Braam, 'this whole story' had its beginnings in the town of Parys, where his mother supported the family with her ladies' boutique and 'taught us about business'. He was about 12 when the family moved to George after his mother decided that she wanted to live in that part of the country, and once again she opened a ladies' boutique.

After studying at Stellenbosch University and completing his military service, Braam followed in his mother's footsteps by opening a small store 'in Mossel Bay, of all places,' in 1989. At first the staff consisted only of Braam and two assistants. But luck was on his side when the government decided that it was time to launch the Mossgas project, and suddenly 10 000 contract workers descended on Mossel Bay. Fortunately his mother was on the ball and reacted quickly, he recounts, 'and she made sure that we stocked the right kind of trousers, shoes and shirts for that market in our store'.

Their average daily turnover was between R500 and R600 at the time. Braam says that he will never forget that Friday in January 1990 when he already had R600 on the cash register at two in the afternoon. Two and a half hours later, the amount came to R19 600. 'It was just incredible when all those people received their first salaries and totally overwhelmed us.' But the comical side, he adds, was that 'I naturally expected a week later that this was what every Friday would look like, because I didn't realise at the time that they were only being paid every two weeks'. But thereafter his store 'was ready for them on a fortnightly basis'.

Tekkie Town was started in 2001, but Braam's breakthrough came with his first big transaction in 1999. When I ask him how this deal came about, Braam explains that, while visiting Port Elizabeth to watch a cricket match, he stayed with his good friend Martin Nefdt, who was an Adidas agent at the time. The agent for Caterpillar shoes asked him to pay a visit to their principal, David Palmer of Medicus Shoes, 'and I thought I might perhaps buy 50 or 100 pairs of shoes from him for the two stores I had at that time'. At Palmer's showroom, he showed Braam examples of what was available and put the inventory down in front of him. When Braam skimmed through the inventory, he realised that the total number came to about 12 000 pairs of shoes. This was much more than he could sell through his two stores.

According to Braam, he was wracking his brains, wondering what he could do with so many shoes, when he suddenly thought of his friend who had been doing business with the cooperatives for years. And, on the spur of the moment, 'without thinking', he offered Palmer R1.2 million for all the shoes. 'There was a silence,' Braam recalls, 'and then he said to me, snootily, "You must be crazy." After a further silence, he asked: "But how are you going to pay me?" And, quite cockily, I told him, "I'll pay you tomorrow", while thinking to myself, What have you just said? Where are you going to get the money to pay him the following day?'

That evening, Braam told his friend about his possible transaction to obtain the 12 000 pairs of Caterpillar shoes and explained his dilemma: he either had to pay Palmer the following day, 'or I had to turn tail and run'. His friend had a solution: Braam could draw a cheque at an ATM by using his home-loan account. At the time, Braam had two home loans for flats in his name. 'I remember that we were in Russell Street in Port Elizabeth at around midnight, and I found out how to transfer money from a home-loan account to my account.' They left with two ATM cheques, each to the value of about R450 000. But he still needed more money. A week or so previously, Braam had sold his only commercial building for R1.3 million, and the buyer owed him a deposit of R300 000. He asked the buyer to pay that amount into Medicus Shoes' account and fax him the deposit slip. 'So, the next day, I arrived at Medicus Shoes with a deposit slip and two ATM cheques, and I had my 12 000 pairs of shoes.'

To me, this first big transaction highlights two things. Not only did Braam see an opportunity in the situation, he was also prepared to risk his own capital on this opportunity. When he talks later about people having to make sure whether or not are they entrepreneurs, I reckon it is this principle that comes to the fore. Everyone constantly sees opportunities; the difference lies in spotting the right opportunity and then being prepared to put your own capital at stake in order to seize it.

And did he manage to sell that mountain of shoes successfully? Braam admits that he was very scared at first and wondered 'how the hell we were going to do it', but with the help of Martin Nefdt ('a fantastic Springbok cyclist in his day' and 'a salesman of note') they sold the lot within about three months.

Braam confesses that 'when we did that wholesale deal, I really thought that I was now a big businessman. At the time, we had no idea of where we would end up.' He opened the first Tekkie Town store in Somerset West, and they decided they 'wanted to focus a bit on the shoe side'. They didn't really go looking for new premises, but saw premises in Goodwood and then heard about suitable premises in Bellville, and each time 'we did another store'.

Out of all the people I interviewed, Braam was probably the one who appeared to be the most surprised by what he had achieved. Throughout our conversation I got the impression that he doesn't seem to realise exactly how successful Tekkie Town is, and that, even now, he still doesn't quite know what has hit him.

I asked Braam why, after growing fairly slowly up to 2008, Tekkie Town suddenly opened 45 stores in that year. The only reason he can think of, he says, is that there was a lot of empty space available in some shopping centres because of the financial crisis, and they had identified the opportunity. 'We bit off more than we could chew,' he admits, 'but, as they say, "If you bite off more than you can chew, you chew like hell", and we pressed on. I remember that on the last Friday in November, we opened nine stores in one day.'

Tekkie Town started with two people and capital of R25 000. Twelve years later, this sport and lifestyle shoe chain, which sells branded footwear at affordable prices, has grown into a business with a turnover of about R1 billion, 220 stores and more than 2 000 employees. To what does Braam attribute this phenomenal success? He 'would firstly say perhaps a great deal of grace'. He and his team are often almost shocked when they look back, because they never expected their business to grow to its present size. When he looks at the opportunities that Africa now offers them, Braam says, 'I shudder to think where all of this is going to end'. He sees enormous opportunities in countries like Nigeria, Kenya and many more, which would 'actually make South Africa seem small'.

When business is in your blood, you realise that things like working hours should not stand in the way of an opportunity to do good business. Hence it is quite normal for this born retailer to conduct business whenever there are enough customers and sales transactions to conclude. Braam illustrates this philosophy with the example of a store next to theirs in Mossel Bay, which closed its doors at noon on 24 December, just when everyone was rushing around to get their last Christmas shopping done. 'Obviously we picked up most of those customers, and they came into our store instead for their purchases.' As Braam puts it, 'business hours don't exist in our books'.

After the interview, we found out that Braam still wanted to go and purchase a bunch of flowers with which he intended to surprise one of his branch managers in Durban. Just before the interview, he had learnt that it was her birthday, and to him it was a logical decision to arrive with flowers when he visited the store. Given this absolute involvement in the business, he should perhaps be less surprised at his success.

When we said goodbye, he handed out his telephone number to the members of the technical team and invited all of us to contact him the next time we walked past a Tekkie Town store; he would make sure that we got a good deal. Braam is indeed a shopkeeper of stature!

BUILDING BLOCKS FOR GROWTH

Lessons from Tekkie Town's growth from one outlet to 220 stores over a period of 12 years:

- **On the financial side** – 'We always adhered to the policy that if there was no money to open new stores, we didn't open them.'
- **Your fundamental aspects have to be in place** – Your personnel aspects, premises and risk management have to be right. 'You can't grow at a faster rate than what your systems allow.'

ADVICE TO ENTREPRENEURS

- You should understand yourself and know whether you can and want to be an entrepreneur.
- In the initial stages, put every cent you make back into the business. 'Don't spend money on cars and houses and eating out and holidays. It's your fertiliser money that should be ploughed back into your business. Later on you will get the opportunity to buy all those things and much more.'

CHAPTER 32

Herman Mashaba

CO-FOUNDER OF BLACK LIKE ME
Interview broadcast on 26 August 2012

Herman grew up in difficult circumstances in the village of GaRamotse in Hammanskraal outside Pretoria. After starting his business career by selling a variety of products on a commission basis, he co-founded the Black Like Me beauty products group in 1985. Herman later sold the successful business and is now, among other positions, chief executive of Leswikeng Minerals & Energy Limited and chairman of the Free Market Foundation.

was very keen to talk to Herman. His is an inspirational story of someone from wretched circumstances who built up a successful business in an extremely hostile environment. Besides having to contend with poverty, a lack of formal education and the then unfavourable business conditions for black entrepreneurs, he had to forge his own path without any family support.

I contacted Herman to request an opportunity to discuss a possible interview on *Sakegesprek*. Because Herman doesn't speak Afrikaans, he was not familiar with the kykNET channel, let alone the programme; nonetheless he agreed to meet me and also to do an interview. The challenge was how we would deal with the language issue. The joint decision was that I would go through the topics with him beforehand. He reckoned he would be able to gather enough from my Afrikaans questions to at least identify the correct topic for his answer. I undertook to repeat any question in English if I detected that he was floundering or had misunderstood a question. In the end we shot the entire interview without it proving necessary to repeat a single question or redo any answer.

We started our conversation with Herman's early years in the 'small village' of GaRamotse in Hammanskraal, 'really directly opposite the industrial area'. His mother was a single parent who worked in Johannesburg as a domestic worker.

One thing that stood out throughout the interview was the principle that you have to take charge of your own destiny. Although his circumstances were difficult, Herman believed that he had to take charge of his life, and he regards this as a deliberate decision that he took at quite an early age. To him, it was a question of personal dignity; from a young age he had heard family members and others in his community speak of 'the loss of personal dignity' they were subjected to. In his teenage years, some of his peers used to go to the white suburbs of Pretoria to earn money as golf caddies or gardeners. 'I actually decided to stay away to make sure that I protect my dignity, because I felt that this was the only thing I had.' When he reflects on his life, Herman says, 'I think that decision really helped me to overcome some of the challenges.'

His peers who were prepared to do casual work in the white suburbs at least came home with a rand or two, but 'what about people like us who stayed behind in the townships?' According to Herman, 'unfortunately I turned into a gambler because I needed money as well'. Education was important to him, and, as he had to get by without parents to support him, 'when I gambled during weekends I would always make sure that I put some money aside to help me get through the week'. While 'gambling really became my salvation', Herman says, 'when I reflect on that upbringing, I think I was very fortunate that I survived.'

After school Herman enrolled for a BAdmin degree at the then University of the North, but had to abandon his studies in his second year when the university was closed temporarily in 1980 as a result of political unrest. In these years he met his wife, Connie, who has been a pillar of strength in his life. In fact, he attributes much of his later success to the fact that he got married to the right woman at an early age. 'I was 22, Connie was 20, and in March this year we celebrated 30 years of marriage.'

Herman worked for a salary for only 30 months of his life: seven months in a clerical job at Spar and 23 months at Motani Industries. During his stint at Motani, he managed to buy a car, and two months later he resigned to follow an independent route and start his own business career. For about two years he sold different products on a commission basis from the boot of his car. He ended up selling hair products as a commission sales rep for a Johannesburg company called The World of Hair. Herman's exposure to the haircare industry made him realise that it offered an excellent opportunity for a business of his own. He concluded that it was a growing industry, and that there was a market for hair products that met the specific needs of black consumers.

'I decided to be proactive before something goes wrong, because I have always been a very proactive person. I take charge of my life all the time,' Herman says. Since he lacked the technical expertise to manufacture hair products himself, he 'took a chance' and asked a production manager at the firm, Johan Kriel, 'an Afrikaner from Boksburg, for that matter', to start a company with him and a fellow salesman: Johan had the knowledge to develop and manufacture the products, and Herman and his colleague would sell them.

Naturally, they did not have many options in those days when it came to raising capital to transform their plan into a business. They submitted their business plan to Walter Dube, a businessman from Mabopane, and persuaded him, after a few meetings, to invest the R30 000 they required. When he looks back at the start of their business, Herman says, it was to him 'such a momentous moment' that they, as 'two young black guys', managed to get 'a white Afrikaner' to join forces with them to form a company. 'Actually, I think our story is a typical case study that this country can look at, because we were all businesspeople, we were capitalists, we really wanted to make money and work within the legal framework, and we took that decision.'

The Black Like Me company was an enormous success. In 1991 Herman decided to exchange Hammanskraal for a house in Heatherdale in Pretoria North, a so-called white suburb. Shortly before he was due to move in, however, a friend showed him an article in an Afrikaans newspaper about 'the storm' his house purchase had created. According to Herman, there was apparently an arrangement in the area at the time that property would not be sold to blacks, and 'right wingers' had marched against the person who had sold him the house. As luck would have it, one of his neighbours turned out to be Pik Botha, the then Minister of Foreign Affairs, who welcomed the new arrivals with a cocktail party at his house. Herman reckons that this welcome probably helped to ensure that he had no trouble from people who were opposed to his presence in the suburb. In his opinion, 'the problem with what happened in the old regime was the misinformation by the political leadership. That's something I'm now fighting about in our new dispensation, to ensure that we don't have the political leadership that divides us as people.'

In 1993 Herman had to overcome a huge setback after his factory burnt down one night. Recalling this 'tragic event in our lives', he describes what a shock it was to watch the flames and to realise that they could salvage nothing from the building. But although he had lost a lot of money, 'I decided that I'm not going to let my dream evaporate in this fire. Fortunately I had a national brand that was strong and well known, and I decided I'm going to rebuild this.' What counted in his favour, he reckons, was 'the culture of saving' he acquired in his youth and still considers very important today. Thanks to 'some reserves' he had, Herman was able to buy a new factory in Midrand, but the process of rebuilding the business proved to be tough. In those days, it was also difficult for him as a black businessman to obtain financing from banks to help with the company's immediate cash-flow needs.

Turning the conversation to present-day South Africa, I asked Herman for his views on our challenges and opportunities. He states frankly that, although we find ourselves 'in a very precarious environment at the moment in our country', he is 'still very positive'. That is also the reason why he is chairman of the Free Market Foundation. Many people hold the view 'that capitalism is not a moral environment', but, as a strong advocate of the capitalist system, he believes that 'if you look at the whole world and the history of mankind, this is the only system that has ever created wealth and prosperity, that created the future for human beings'. As far as his own life is concerned, Herman believes he has achieved success through self-reliance, a thirst for knowledge and the realisation that it is his responsibility 'to work for myself and my family and not really rely on other people'. 'That is the kind of system I prefer.' While he does see threats to the capitalist system in South Africa, 'at the same time I believe that, as members of civil society, we should really engage our political leadership to ensure that they don't interfere with the system, because any other system can only be a disaster for the future of our country'.

What would he emphasise if he had to advise young people about opportunities and what they can do to prepare themselves for the future? According to Herman, he 'keeps harping on this whole idea of you as an individual', who has to take personal responsibility for your life, regardless of your background, your race or your gender. Parents and the rest of society have the responsibility to ensure that children receive the best possible education, 'because without proper, effective education we are risking the future going forward'. Once young people have been given that education, however, he believes that it's up to them to understand that they really have to take personal responsibility for their future. In his view, the country offers 'a wide range of opportunities' to young people. Instead of prescribing a specific field or sector, he would suggest that 'it's up to you as an individual to decide what actually makes you tick, and then use that as an opportunity'.

Herman returns to the importance of education and stresses that while 'formal education is key', young people should not restrict themselves to formal studies and have to keep on educating themselves. In Herman's own case, his academic studies were disrupted, 'but I decided to educate myself and that's what I do'. He reads as much as he can, he says, and talks to experts to acquire knowledge about issues he has to deal with. His advice to young people in this regard is to 'educate yourself by making sure that you mix with the right people. Read the books you enjoy, but read, read, read to gain the necessary knowledge.'

You can't help admiring Herman. He could hardly have found himself in less favourable circumstances, yet he has made a success of his life. What stood out from the conversation is his principle that you should never allow your circumstances to dictate where you are headed; it comes down to a conscious decision, a decision to take charge of your own future.

After the interview, Herman contacted me and said he never knew that so many of his friends and business partners watched the programme, and that in Afrikaans!

WHAT QUALITIES DOES AN ENTREPRENEUR NEED TO SUCCEED DESPITE DIFFICULT CIRCUMSTANCES?

- You must take responsibility for your future and take charge of your own destiny.
- Don't rely on someone else to do things for you.
- Make sure that you get a good education if your circumstances allow it. Build on your formal education for the rest of your life through self-education.

CHAPTER 33

Jan Nelson

CHIEF EXECUTIVE OF PAN AFRICAN RESOURCES

Interview broadcast on 2 September 2012

Jan grew up in Johannesburg and qualified almost accidentally as a geologist at the then Rand Afrikaans University (RAU, now the University of Johannesburg). After a career in exploration and mining at several of the larger mining groups, he decided to join a junior mining group with serious cash-flow problems. Since assuming the position of chief executive in 2005, Jan has overseen the transformation of Pan African Resources into one of the stronger and more thriving junior groups, with a market value of R5 billion.

When I interviewed Bernard Swanepoel, former CEO of the Harmony gold-mining group and now at the helm of the Village Main Reef mining group, he referred specifically to Jan as one of the country's bright young mine bosses. South Africa's mining landscape is dotted with fascinating personalities, and there are more than enough with dubious reputations. In such an environment, you have to make your choices with discretion.

As with any interview, you do your homework beforehand with regard to your prospective guest. Because it concerned the mining sector, I was even more wary. Apart from Bernard's recommendation, I contacted some of the bankers and analysts who specialise in the mining sector. The unanimous verdict was that Jan Nelson is regarded as a quality individual and a miner who does business honestly.

Jan landed in mining by chance. He actually wanted to study marine biology, but when he arrived at RAU and was told 'you can't make money from marine biology, I got a fright'. The only department that still had places available was Geology. When a professor's explanation of 'how the plates of the earth move and collide, volcanoes and that type of thing' captured his imagination, Jan was hooked.

In retrospect, he is pleased with this decision to focus on geology. While there are many different fields of expertise in the mining industry, from finance and management to mining engineering, he would definitely recommend geology as a field of study to young people who want to enter mining, Jan says. 'Mining is about the ore body, and it all starts with geology.' As one advances in the mining industry, there are always opportunities to diversify into other directions.

Jan worked at several of the larger and more prominent mining groups, yet in 2005 he accepted the position of chief executive at the small and near-bankrupt Pan African Resources. To understand this decision, I started by asking him about the job interview. According to Jan, his interview with Rob Still and Anton Esterhuizen went more or less as follows: 'Listen, Jan, the company only has enough cash for three months. We have two projects. Both of them are bad. You'll have to get rid of them. If you're game for it, do you want the job?' Because he was acquainted with Still and Esterhuizen, and knew how they built up small companies, Jan decided that 'this is a wonderful opportunity, let's give it a chance'.

Most people would reject an offer like this out of hand – who would want a job in a company with two dodgy assets and cash for only three months? Jan, however, saw it as an opportunity instead of a huge risk. What motivated his decision? To be honest, he admits, his response was 'probably impulsive' because they insisted on an immediate answer. But he reckons that there was also a backdrop to the decision. At that stage, after a long time with large mining companies, he had started doing consulting work on his own. He thus had the idea in the back of his mind that he wanted to his own thing, 'but when I got this opportunity, I told myself I couldn't let it slip by'.

How did he, as newly appointed CEO, tackle the challenge of getting Pan African Resources on its feet? The first thing that had to be done, he says, was to assess the two projects and decide on their merits. One was 'not so good' and they disposed of it, but the other was a good project. 'We decided to continue with it, but of course we didn't have enough money to do so.' Jan recounts how he had to do the rounds of fund managers in London, begging for money, virtually on his hands and knees. He was unknown to the fund managers and had no record of having done anything like this before, 'so the guys aren't actually interested in seeing you'. But with the help of 'friends and family' in the UK he managed to obtain about £400 000. 'Then I could do some work again, and things continued in this vein for about a year or two.'

The easy way out would have been to throw in the towel and realise that he had made an error of judgement. When I ask whether he ever lost courage during those early days, Jan replies emphatically: 'No – no.' He attributes his perseverance to the fact that the company had a good project and he enjoyed the support of directors, a passionate chairman and many friends. 'You must just never give up. It became tough at times, but I think that's what makes it enjoyable when you look back now after four or five years.' Besides, Jan adds, 'the more people tell me that I can't do it or that it won't work, the more obstinate I tend to get about showing them that we can'.

When one looks back on turnaround successes like that of Pan African Resources, there are usually some turning points that made the eventual transformation possible. In their case, the breakthrough came when the company bought the Barberton gold mine from Metorex. 'That was when we turned ourselves around completely. It gave us production and cash flow, but it all happened with the help of a group of people – it wasn't only me,' Jan says modestly. 'It was a whole team that brought it about.'

Today Pan African Resources is a successful company worth R5 billion in a sector that is struggling. What did they do right? The first factor he highlights is that they have a fairly enterprising board that 'keeps our feet on the ground' and gets them to focus on their cash flow. 'Even when you get more cash, or already have enough of it, you still need to count every cent.' Among other factors that contributed to their success, he singles out 'a good team' and 'a good network'. According to Jan, 'we built up a network of people who supported us, because they saw that that which we had promised and which we did, worked'. He emphasises again that 'you have to keep both feet on the ground. You should never become too big-headed.'

It was clear throughout the interview that Jan is positive about the junior mining sector in South Africa, despite the persistently negative reports in some of the media. Why this optimism? Jan brims with enthusiasm when he talks about the sector. 'I think that there's an enormous future in the junior sector in South Africa. If I was one of the big guys – and perhaps I should now choose my words carefully – I'd be worried, because their assets are reaching the end of their economic lives. They must produce a certain number of ounces to cover their overhead costs, and this is where the opportunities now start emerging for the juniors. There's a whole industry that's opening up for us, and I believe you're now looking at guys that want to consolidate. The one guy buys an asset from the other guy.' He reckons that junior mining is an extremely exciting sector to be in, and that it is likely to see 'incredible growth' in South Africa in the next five years.

When it comes to his views on managing people, Jan observes that they have 'a very flat structure'. Everyone has a contribution to make and an opinion from which you can learn something. As a leader, 'you have to listen to your people and give them the chance to give their input. It's actually easy to manage an organisation if you just open your ears.'

There were two things in particular that stayed in my mind after the interview. Firstly, I think few people would have seen the initial job offer as an opportunity, yet Jan not only spotted the opportunity, he jumped at it. Secondly, if you believe in your dream, you should never give up hope – even if you get nine 'no's', the tenth response may be the 'yes', and you only need one 'yes'.

If South Africa's next generation of mine bosses should consist of more Jan Nelsons, mining is headed for a rosy future.

ADVICE ON MANAGING A BUSINESS OUT OF DIFFICULT CIRCUMSTANCES

- **You must have a dream** – 'You must be able to see what you want to do and then you have to pursue it.'
- **You must never give up hope** – 'You'll always get someone who will tell you why it can't work.'
- **You must stay realistic and listen** to 'some of the things, but you just have to tell yourself, "I can do it"; and if you have a good plan, a good dream and vision, and the right people, you can do it'.
- **You must never throw in the towel.**

WHY JAN WOULD RECOMMEND A CAREER IN THE MINING INDUSTRY

- It offers so many opportunities in different fields, 'from financing to geology, metallurgy, health and the environment, and it's an incredibly practical industry'.
- You can see what you are doing and how things are happening. 'You can see how you create jobs, how we build something, and I think that is what's so wonderful about the industry.'

CHAPTER 34

Adriaan Scheeres

CO-FOUNDER AND CHIEF EXECUTIVE OF PRAGMA

Interview broadcast on 9 September 2012

Adriaan holds a degree in Industrial Engineering from Stellenbosch University as well as a master's degree in Information Systems. He and a colleague started the Pragma engineering group, which specialises in physical asset management. Twenty years later, Pragma has a turnover of more than R300 million and employs over 340 people in offices in South Africa, Brazil and China.

The interview was to take place at Pragma's offices in Durbanville. On our arrival, the team was faced with a technical conundrum. Adriaan is the tallest person I have ever encountered – easily over seven feet, according to the old system. We were not surprised when he remarked that he had won a competition for the tallest man in the Cape in 1983. The challenge in terms of good television was to position Adriaan and me in such a way that we could converse with our heads more or less at the same level. After some experimentation with chairs and a few cushions, this goal was eventually achieved.

A portrait of Adriaan's grandfather hangs on the wall in his office. The reason for this becomes clear as we start talking about the origins of his desire to start his own business. The idea of starting his own enterprise was already with him by the time he entered university, says Adriaan. This mindset was inculcated by his Dutch grandfather, who came to South Africa after the Second World War and ran a carpentry business. 'Every holiday that I worked at his business, he instilled it in me: it's best to start your own business and do your own thing.'

Deciding to start your own enterprise is one thing; the challenge is to convert that plan into a fully fledged business. How did it work in Adriaan's case? As a good engineer, one is taught that there has to be 'a solid plan', he says. Hence he and his team devoted much time to testing their idea in the market. What Adriaan considered crucial for success, however, was 'choosing good partners'. He and his partner, Arnold Botha, first defined the business and then launched it. Adriaan also regards it as very important that, especially in the initial years, 'we measured ourselves monthly and annually and stayed focused on our idea in the market'. There are many things that can make you drift off course when you start a business. Adriaan reckons they owe their success to the fact that 'we said we wanted to provide services in the maintenance environment, and we concentrated on that and were very focused in the execution of our plan'.

The plan has developed over the past 20 years into the Pragma group of companies, but what exactly does Pragma do, and who are their clients? According to Adriaan, 'every industry out there is our client' because they all have assets and those assets have to be used efficiently so that people can be successful in, for example, a manufacturing process or a transport business. But Pragma focuses specifically on five industries: mining, the power distribution and supply industry, original equipment manufacturers (OEMs), the high-speed manufacturing industry and what they call distribution facilities. The last-mentioned are companies such as Shell and Shoprite that have many facilities and assets all over the country. The services delivered by Pragma are aimed at improving the reliability and availability of clients' physical assets. Adriaan says that they are not a consultancy: 'We have converted our products into services. So we contract with an owner a certain reliability, a certain availability, a certain life-cycle cost.'

Pragma as it is today – was that his plan and dream? Adriaan hesitates a moment before he replies: 'Yes and no.' The dream was to have a business of his own; Pragma started as a consultancy and later embarked on services and products, 'but the dream grew and you always need a dream to drive you'. After ten years, the dream grew bigger: to expand internationally. And after about 15 years, 'we told ourselves that we really have a product and a service that makes sense to the industry out there'. According to Adriaan, this is where the idea originated of focusing on the Brics countries (Brazil, Russia, India, China, South Africa) and why Pragma started expanding in these markets.

With Pragma now having offices in South Africa, Brazil and China, it is clear that this focus works. But why specifically target the Brics countries? Adriaan says it is not that they don't feel equal to tackling more advanced markets, such as Europe, Australia or the United States, 'but our products and services also work very well in developing countries'. Africa, including South Africa, doesn't have a very good history when it comes to maintaining infrastructure and equipment, and the same goes for Brazil and China. These are all growing countries, 'so we told ourselves that we would like to focus on the Brics countries'.

Pragma currently employs more than 340 people worldwide, many of whom were trained in South Africa. What are Adriaan's views on the quality of South African engineers, particularly from his own experience? He answers my question by firstly explaining that Pragma decided they wouldn't necessarily take South African engineers to Brazil or China because language, for one, is a problem. They 'packaged' their services 'very neatly', translated the packaged version, and train engineers in Brazil and China to be able to deliver services in those countries in accordance with Pragma's methodology. As far as South African engineers are concerned, Adriaan describes them as 'a sought-after species' that one finds all over the world. The reason for this, he reckons, is their work ethic and their creativity. 'In my years at Iscor,' he says, 'we worked at the railways, we received our training at Armscor, and the expertise that was built up there is in high demand worldwide.'

His answer highlights the principle that Pragma is a people business; the individuals they employ *are* the business. The consequence is that the business walks out of the door every afternoon and then hopefully walks in again the next morning. How do they make sure that they get the right people for their business? When the company was younger, Adriaan says, they had a specific recruitment strategy where people in the business were asked to bring in good engineers with whom they had worked before. Today the top and middle management of Pragma 'are almost all what I call hand-picked guys' with whom he mostly also had personal interviews to see whether they would fit into the culture and value system and could work in an entrepreneurial environment. According to Adriaan, Pragma's 'greatest success is people who enter from below'. Every year they appoint about five to eight young, newly qualified engineers 'from across the country, all colours, etc'. These newcomers 'are then trained from scratch and they start growing within the company'.

Attracting the right people is one thing, but the challenge is to retain them and to ensure that these highly qualified individuals want to return every day. Because engineers are so sought after and regularly get other offers, Pragma developed 'a very specific strategy to keep people happy'. Firstly, says Adriaan, it is important to create a very specific culture. The culture and the value system, into which people have to fit, promote cohesion and hold them together. Secondly, they devote much time and attention to training. Adriaan personally drives leadership training within the organisation, and they have an internal training programme for senior engineers and senior management. While external people play a role in the programme, as mentors, trainers and motivators, Adriaan says that he personally spends a great deal of time with these leaders 'so that they can transfer the culture, the essence of the business, to the rest'.

In conclusion, I wanted to get an informed opinion on South Africa's physical assets and the real state of our engineering infrastructure from someone in the know, who works with it on a daily basis. According to Adriaan, our physical assets are at this stage still in a good condition, but he uses the 2009 election as an illustration of the problem we have: 'The whole election was basically about poor service delivery, and people tried to make capital out of who is to be blamed for that.' There is enough money available, he says, 'but not enough money is being spent in the right places, and at the right time, to maintain our assets'.

What is required, in his view, to improve this situation? Adriaan stresses, firstly, the importance of defining what needs to be done in order to maintain those assets. This is often a problem, 'because the old guard have disappeared from the system' and consequently the new management don't really have an idea of what has to be done with regard to maintenance. A second challenge is that the money and the contractors who have to supply and maintain those assets 'should be channelled properly so that the money is used only for fixing that asset and not for all sorts of other things'.

What strikes me about this interview with Adriaan is that he is an entrepreneur who identified a specific challenge and then built a business around this challenge. I am convinced that we would solve many of our problems if we allow entrepreneurs, like Adriaan and his colleagues, to assist with the formulation and implementation of solutions.

FOUR CORE PRINCIPLES FOR CONVERTING A BUSINESS PLAN INTO A SUCCESSFUL BUSINESS

- **Focus** – 'To me, it's incredibly important that people should choose a business plan and should focus on getting that plan implemented.'
- **Time and patienc**e – Adriaan equates the principle of time with a good long-term investment. 'I've seen so many young engineers or young entrepreneurs – the day he starts a business, he thinks he's a rich man and he now has to drive a big car and have a big house.' Along with this, he emphasises patience: 'You really have to be patient and, step by step, make sure that you grow.'
- **Choose the right partners** – 'Not a nice pal, but a partner who can complement your weak points and who can support you.' And when you appoint young people, 'don't appoint people for reasons such as feeling sorry for them, but because they can really let the business grow for you'.
- **Create a culture** in the business 'within which people feel comfortable and enjoy working'. He adds that 'a culture is something you create; it doesn't just happen, you can plan it'. And then you have to make sure that the culture is 'a proven thing that you can measure and manage within the organisation'.

CHAPTER 35

Santie Botha

FORMERLY AT ABSA AND MTN, NOW DIRECTOR OF COMPANIES
Interview broadcast on 16 September 2012

After graduating from Stellenbosch University, Santie worked at Unilever, where she gained experience in the marketing division of a world leader in the consumer goods sector. In 1996 Santie joined the Absa Group, and she is credited with the integration and establishment of the Absa brand. After seven years at Absa, she joined MTN as an executive director, where she was responsible for establishing the MTN brand in 21 countries. Santie was named South Africa's Businesswoman of the Year in 2010.

She left MTN in 2010 and currently serves as non-executive director on the boards of several listed companies, including the private education group Curro (chairperson), Imperial Holdings, Tiger Brands, Telkom and Famous Brands. Santie is also the chancellor of the Nelson Mandela Metropolitan University.

Banking has always been an industry where men rule the roost, whether in South Africa or the rest of the world. Add to this the fairly conservative Afrikaans culture, and one can imagine an environment that might be rather hostile and aloof for a woman.

In 1996 Santie joined the Absa Group, which at that stage still had different brands with their own identities and traditions. By the time she left, seven years later, the unified Absa brand had become so solidly entrenched that South Africans now consider it one of the country's iconic brands.

I started off our conversation with Santie's move to Absa in 1996, and asked her about her first experiences. Her biggest challenge, she says, 'was to build up credibility within the bank, because you were dealing with bankers who had been there for 30, 40 years. They had grown up in the bank.' Besides being young, she was the first woman to be appointed on a senior management level, and, on top of that, her experience was in consumer goods, not banking. Hence there was an attitude of, 'What can you possibly teach us?' Santie explains that, while she was 'half appointed as a change agent' at that stage, it was also very important to her 'to really understand the heart and soul of the bank'. Volkskas, Allied, United and Trust Bank all had their own distinctive cultures, with some more Afrikaans and others more English, and the challenge was to understand 'where people were coming from' and 'how they wanted to see the bank grow'.

Being appointed was one thing, but taking the decisions and implementing them was something else altogether. Santie's task was to decide whether the four banking brands would continue to exist or should be combined into a new, single brand. For this process to have any chance of success, she had to convince the senior people and win their support. How does one approach such a task?

Santie recounts how she drew up her own questionnaire and interviewed senior people sometimes up to four times, 'just to make sure that I really understood what had to be done'. Opinions were divided. There were ardent supporters of a single brand, but 'then you had another camp, at a very senior level, who said: "Under no circumstances are you going to touch any of these four brands of ours. You're a newcomer, and Volkskas is an established institution in this rural town. My grandfather, my uncle and my aunt all bank at this bank, and there's a history."' And because there is always intense emotion around brands, 'it was crucial to get everyone on the same page'.

Santie points out how extremely complex the brand-changing process was. 'In business, people often say that it was one person who did it, but that's never the case.' When you're talking about a bank, you're dealing with risk, she says, and they had to consider the risk attached to a new brand when the existing four brands together had a brand equity of more than 400 years. On the other hand, they had four different retail banks, each with its own identity, that were in competition with one another. 'The big question was: if we had to move to a single brand, what would the implications be, particularly from an IT systems angle?' The approach she followed was to look at the risk of a single brand but also at the benefits for the future, such as the cost savings they would achieve. The 'big message' they wanted to get across to people was that a single brand 'is better for the market, it's better for business. You are more focused. You have a bigger vision.' It was through this message that they had to get everyone at a senior level 'to share the same vision'.

She refers to the 'great amount of homework' that was done to substantiate the single-brand view, and to the processes that were followed to convince the staff of the benefits and get them to buy into the idea. In the case of big projects, 'you always have to get support from the bottom to the very top'. What was most important to her was to get the best people on the team who had to make this project work, at all levels in the bank. When you 'take big leaps' in business, Santie explains, 'your people, especially at branch level at that stage, say, "But what happens to me?"' The 'big promise' they made to the employees was that this step was not aimed at reducing staff numbers; it was to the benefit of the bank in terms of 'where we wanted to take this group'.

When I look back on what Santie has achieved and the success of the Absa brand today, the adoption of a single brand makes complete sense, and it seems as if the process couldn't have had any other logical outcome. Perhaps it is precisely because she managed the process so well that it feels as if Absa has always been a part of the South African landscape. To Santie, it was 'a miracle' that Absa was voted South Africa's most-loved financial services brand after only three years.

Santie shocked the market when she left a highly successful career at Absa after seven years and joined the MTN Group as an executive director. Banking and telecommunications are worlds apart – how did she experience these differences? According to Santie, the major difference between the two industries is that, in financial services, where you deal with risk and people's money, 'you have to be extremely cautious when it comes to phenomenal innovations you may want to rush into'. In telecommunications, on the other hand, you can 'implement ten innovations every day if you want to, but it is about what you choose to do'. In terms of marketing principles, however, there is little difference between the two industries. 'You're still dealing with a customer, with a brand, and with customer service.'

The challenge that awaited her at MTN was different from what it had been at Absa; at that stage, the MTN Group was involved in only six countries, with big plans for the rest of Africa and the Middle East. At their first marketing and sales strategy conference, Santie says, she told her colleagues in the team that 'this isn't a group conference, it's a global conference'. They were now looking at business in terms of everything they wanted to do in Africa, because they had global aspirations and intended changing their vision to say that they wanted to be the leading telecommunications business in developing countries. From a marketing perspective, the chief executives and the marketing directors specifically asked what needed to be done and how one could ensure that everyone shared the same vision. Every 'MTN way of doing things' was totally different in the countries where they already had a presence, and one was faced with 'the not-invented-here syndrome'. In Nigeria, for example, she was told, 'No, no, Santie, you don't understand. This is how we do things here.' But once they began implementing 'the global principles and everyone started buying into the bigger vision, it was fairly easy'.

When one considers these two major projects, I reckon there is probably no marketing person during the past decades who has achieved what Santie managed to pull off. In the most conservative sector she did away with four long-established financial services brands and made a new brand a household name. Then, on top of that, she built the MTN brand to the point where the company became one of the sponsors of the 2010 Fifa World Cup.

We concluded our conversation by touching on her view of South Africa and the future. Santie emphasises that she wants to continue 'making a positive contribution towards exploiting this enormous potential we have in South Africa and Africa. If we as South Africans and Africans don't do it, someone else will do it for us, and we definitely cannot allow that.'

I am convinced that Santie herself will play a big part in ensuring that Africa and South Africa will be developed by ourselves – she simply has too much vitality and drive to leave it up to others!

MANAGEMENT PRINCIPLES

- Every person has to decide what his or her priorities are and then make sure that the employer understands their priorities.
- Every person is responsible for his or her own career success, not the employer. 'If you just do things randomly, without a plan, things will also happen to you randomly.'

- On leadership – 'Leaders are never alone. Good leaders surround themselves with brilliant people who are specialists in their fields and come from diverse backgrounds, and they have the ability to get the best from this team.'
- On the so-called glass ceiling for women – If you are good enough and it is important enough to you, you will get to the top. 'The glass ceiling is there only if you choose to see it that way.'

CHAPTER 36

Hendrik du Toit

CHIEF EXECUTIVE OF INVESTEC ASSET MANAGEMENT
Interview broadcast on 23 September 2012

Hendrik grew up in Cape Town and holds master's degrees from Stellenbosch University and Cambridge University in the UK. In 1991 he joined Investec and started Investec Asset Management with R200 million under management. Today Investec Asset Management manages assets in excess of R825 billion, with offices and clients across the world. In 2011 Hendrik won the *Funds Europe* award for the European Fund Management Personality of the Year, and in 2012 he was named CEO of the Year at the prestigious *Financial News* awards for excellence in European institutional asset management.

I t was clear from the outset that Hendrik had done his homework about me as well as about the *Sakegesprek* programme. He had watched some of the previous interviews and knew exactly what the numbers and profile of the viewers were. I considered it a compliment when he remarked that he no longer readily granted interviews to some of the international business channels because of the many instances where their background knowledge had been sketchy and their preparation poor. While it was good news that he agreed to do the interview, I knew that I had better not make a hash of it!

I decided to start the conversation with Hendrik's much-discussed first encounter with Stephen Koseff, now chief executive of Investec. Hendrik was an investment analyst at Old Mutual at the time. 'Stephen used to come to us to get capital for his clients, and in this case it was Bidvest,' he recounts. Old Mutual decided to support them and, 'typical of a pushy young analyst, you want to tell the company what to do. We had heated debates about that.' Hendrik describes Stephen as 'a wonderful guy' with whom he has had a very good working relationship over the past 21 years, their 'long debates' and 'many disagreements' notwithstanding.

One day Hendrik received a call from Bernard Kantor, who asked whether he was interested in joining Investec; they wanted to take asset management seriously and were looking for someone to establish Investec Asset Management. 'I immediately said no, but we had lunch together almost every month because he's a very nice guy to chat to, and in the end we decided that there was an opportunity in South Africa.' In those days, asset management was dominated by the insurance companies. Allan Gray was already fairly strong and there were one or two small boutiques, but nothing else. 'So it didn't seem to be a sector one could enter, and maybe that was a lesson to me – everything that looks as if it's filled and as if all the space has already been taken, always has an opening.'

In 1991 Hendrik joined Investec. They started Investec Asset Management with R200 million under management, as a newcomer in a competitive market with established players. The first three years, he says, was 'quite a learning process'. The lesson for him from that time was that he had thought 'asset management is only about managing money. I forgot that you have to get clients and that you need an infrastructure.' According to Hendrik, what they did right was 'to focus on the important things'. They achieved good returns for their existing investors, who supported them with more money. The market suddenly started opening up for a new player. The pivotal factor, in his view, was that they were very positive about the changes in South Africa, 'maybe because we weren't trapped in the paradigms of the past', and a large part of their portfolio was invested in growing companies such as Bidvest and Imperial, which were still small at the time.

Over the next 20 years Investec Asset Management grew from a small start-up to an international business managing more than R825 billion. What did they do right to achieve this phenomenal growth? 'The crucial thing in our business,' he says, 'is that you have to look after your clients. Your clients come first.' A second and 'vital' factor to which Hendrik ascribes their success is that Investec has always had an international agenda. 'Our industry is actually a global industry. It's not only a domestic industry.'

When he looks back on highlights on their growth path, Hendrik says, the first was 'just to get past year one', to get a team together and make 'that first period' work. 'There were wonderful people with us on the journey and many of them are still part of the journey today. So we managed to keep people together. That's the second highlight.' A third highlight was the breakthrough that came when 'we won our first institutional mandate in South Africa. We've always had a unit trust business, but the big institutions didn't really want to work with us.' A fourth and major highlight was 'when we went overseas and we had the courage of our conviction to follow our own mind instead of listening to what the rest of the market said'. And a few years later 'the market started coming to us because we had perhaps read the world a bit more accurately than others'.

The rest, he says, is incremental. 'Asset management is a much more incremental business than something like technology, where with one idea you can advance tremendously.' He refers to Investec Asset Management as the type of business Jim Collins calls the 'hedgehog' in his book *Good to Great*, 'a slow and steady business that has to do things every day and doesn't take big leaps'. 'We don't really have so many highlights and that's why we don't throw big parties when we reach a milestone, because it's merely business as usual,' he remarks.

There are very few fund managers in the southern hemisphere, and even fewer from Africa, who have succeeded in competing successfully on the capital markets in the northern hemisphere. Hendrik reckons that what makes Investec Asset Management very interesting is that they 'actually represent the businesses of the future'. After the financial crisis, we live in a much more equal world when it comes to competition. He uses the example of 'the compliment Apple paid Samsung' by taking them to court. 'Could you have imagined 20 years ago that a Korean company would be vying for dominance in a major industry with one of America's most valuable companies?' At Investec Asset Management they pride themselves on the fact that they are one of the first companies in the services industry that have grown largely organically from a domestic position in an emerging market and succeeded in becoming internationally competitive. 'We see our role now actually as returning, as being an intermediary between emerging and developed worlds' – many of the people who save and the people who build new businesses will be doing business in the southern hemisphere.

Fund managers are usually highly trained specialists with very strong opinions and often also 'egos' that have to be taken into account. In the case of Investec Asset Management, they have 700 investment professionals, based in 13 countries, who provide advice and do business worldwide with clients from 122 countries. How does one manage a set-up like that? Hendrik believes that 'if you have a value system and a culture in a business that people like, they carry on on their own. In our case, we give our people space.' He doesn't see it as his role to dictate to seasoned specialists, such as John Biccard or Clyde Rossouw, how they should manage the money they work with. What does rest with him, though, 'is to see whether they manage funds in the way they initially undertook to do and whether they're doing the necessary work to make good investment decisions, because it's other people's money'. They have 'something of a broad church within Investec Asset Management. People are able to think freely and have the freedom to do what they want to and to develop.' It took them about 15 years to get the phrase 'the space to create' as consensus in the business, he says. 'The last thing you want to do when a business becomes big is to try and manage it from the centre like a puppet master. Then it's bound to fail.'

As far as future trends in the world of investments are concerned, Hendrik is of the view that 'we're entering an incredibly interesting world in which the speed of change will accelerate'. The Western financial crisis has suddenly made people aware of the fact that 'there's a very big world out there', with five billion people who are currently advancing economically and creating opportunities worldwide. 'If you as an investor have your radar screens positioned to search for opportunities across the globe and if you realise that something massive is happening here, you can do extremely well.' We now have 'an inclusive world' instead of 'a Western-dominated world alongside a large poor world with nothing but corruption and coups; that world is past.' The challenge for the future, he adds, is how the planet will be able to support the growing world population and to accommodate all who want to advance economically.

He reckons that 'South Africans who are open-minded' are well equipped for this new world, 'because we understand the combination of developing and developed world and the turbulence of change'. According to Hendrik, it is likely that 'many big businesses can be built, very interesting things can be done' in South Africa over the next ten or 20 years.

What struck me most about the interview was the palpable confidence with which Hendrik dealt with the questions and topics. He was well prepared, walked in and answered my questions, and excused himself in time to catch a flight to one of the 20 offices. One got the impression that, in a changing world with fluctuating markets, Hendrik is in control and won't let bumps like a debt crisis or political instability fluster him.

WHAT MAKES A GOOD INVESTMENT MANAGER?

- A passion for the markets and for investments.
- Independent thinking. 'The ability to stick to his position and not be scared when things are really tough, when he underperforms or when the market is against him.'
- Humility when it is called for. 'To put his pride in his pocket and to say I'm wrong, I now have to change my position because I can't fight against the whole world.'

WHAT IS A GOOD INVESTMENT DECISION?

- 'A good investment decision is so often measured over the first few months, and then everyone gets tremendously excited. That's not how it is done. I think that it only becomes a good investment decision at the selling stage or the acquisition stage. Once you get that income stream which you thought you had bought, or when you sell that asset that you bought for a certain price at a much higher price, then you've made the money.'

BASIC INVESTMENT PRINCIPLES

- **KISS – Keep it simple, stupid**. 'Investments are actually much simpler than people think; avoid anything that is complex.'
- **Get good advice** from someone you can talk to and that you trust. 'Good advice is not that Warren Buffett is going to be your financial adviser.'
- **Focus on the long term** – 'Buy investments of good quality, stick to them and keep it fairly simple.'

CHAPTER 37

Fred Robertson

CO-FOUNDER AND EXECUTIVE DEPUTY CHAIRMAN OF BRIMSTONE

Interview broadcast on 30 September 2012

Fred grew up in Cape Town's District Six. He was 15 when his family was forcibly removed under the Group Areas Act. After studying teaching, he taught for a while, but later joined Old Mutual and started his own insurance broking business in 1990. In 1995 he co-founded Brimstone, a black-controlled and -managed investment company that was listed on the JSE in 1998. Brimstone now boasts a market value of over R3 billion. Besides being a non-executive director of Old Mutual, Fred is, among others, chairman of the Lion of Africa insurance company. In January 2013, after the interview, Fred was appointed as executive chairman of Brimstone.

Fred is very proud of Brimstone, but I think his greatest source of pride is the difference that the success of the company has made to ordinary people's lives – especially to those who bought shares with hard-earned money and are now able to share in the dividends and capital growth.

Our conversation started with Fred's decision to study teaching, and why this decision is still part of the successful businessman of today. Fred reckons that his choice of profession at the time could be ascribed to what had been instilled in him and his classmates during his schooldays at Trafalgar High. They had very good teachers, he says, and what they were taught extended beyond narrow subject knowledge: 'We were taught that we had to make a contribution to society.' Teaching was regarded as a profession through which 'you would help the people in your own community, help to educate them'. He sums up this ethos by referring to the call that was prevalent at the time: 'Each one teach one.'

After teaching for a few years, Fred started working at Old Mutual as an insurance broker. Why did he make that shift? In those days, 'there were restrictions as to what kind of work people from my community could do', he explains, and 'an insurance representative was one of the jobs we could do'. While he was well equipped for the job on account of his communication and writing skills as a teacher, Fred admits that he 'didn't like it very much'. But it was 'a job that put food on the table for me', and he believes that he was quite good at it.

Fred's first job in the business sector was that of an insurance representative at Old Mutual; today he is a non-executive director of the same company. Did he ever imagine at the time that he would end up in such a position? 'No, never,' he says. Fred admits candidly that he has always been a big dreamer, 'but it didn't go as far as dreaming that I'd be a director of Old Mutual one day'.

After ten years at Old Mutual he decided early in 1990 to start his own business as an independent broker, and 'that's where my business life began'. I asked Fred what it was like to run his own insurance broking business as an entrepreneur and what he regards as the factors that made him successful, given that so many small businesses fail. It was just a one-man business, Fred says, and he worked from home. 'I kept a very, very tight rein on my expenses.' He worked all day, and completed his administrative work at night. Among the lessons from those days that have stayed with him are that you have to work hard, you have to believe in your product, and you have to be available to your clients and to treat them well.

The big step came in 1995 with the establishment of Brimstone. Fred founded the company with Mustaq Brey, his accountant at the time. Having a plan was one thing, but raising the capital to execute it was a challenge. According to Fred, they realised that if they wanted to be mainstream business players, they required capital. 'We then went to our community – our friends, our families, our clients – and we explained our dream, our vision and our plan to them.' Some of them believed in the company and bought shares, he says, and they are still shareholders today. 'Others just told us, "No thanks, you'll never make it."' Some of the doubting Thomases later changed their tune and bought shares during the second round. 'We now have more than 3 000 direct shareholders.'

Throughout our conversation, the notion of changing people's lives, of having a positive social impact and of contributing to the betterment of society while doing business constantly comes to the fore. Brimstone, with many shareholders from Fred's circle of friends, decided to list on the JSE in 1998. The listing was a major step, and Fred reckons that it was a significant milestone for the company. They listed Brimstone at Cape Town's Good Hope Centre, which is located on the site of the old District Six fruit and vegetable market. 'We thought it would be nice to show the people we're now taking them from a fruit market to an exchange market. More than a thousand people attended the event, and they all saw how the price of their shares rose.' Fred explained that they had a video link with the JSE, and people 'were able to see how they could sell shares or buy more shares'. In his view, that was in itself an educational process. The listing was also important to Brimstone because they could raise more capital, from a broader market, to do bigger deals. The empowerment symbolism of the venue where the listing took place becomes clear when Fred refers to Brimstone as 'the first company that was started on the Cape Flats and is now listed on the JSE'.

Brimstone now has a market value of more than R3 billion and is a very successful company, with a wide variety of interests. Fred's pride is visible when he talks about the difference Brimstone's success has made to the lives of those first shareholders. As he explains, 'a person who invested R6 000 at the time bought 5 000 shares at the issue price of R1.25 per share. This person has already been paid back his original investment capital in dividends and cash payouts, while the value of the shares that investor still holds now comes to about R120 000,' which includes an interest in the Life Healthcare group. Brimstone shareholders have been receiving dividends for the past eight years, and are now also being paid dividends twice a year from Life Healthcare. 'Whenever dividends are paid, whether from Brimstone or from Life Healthcare, I get many calls and many smiles from the community, and, I must say, it gives one quite a nice feeling.'

To me, the striking feature is the extent to which the company has become an asset for the community, and that this is precisely what upliftment is about. As Fred puts it, they have a genuinely broad-based South African shareholder base that stretches 'from Mitchells Plain to Musina, from Khayelitsha to KZN'. At Brimstone they believe that everyone in the country should be able to benefit from empowerment. The same moral compass that directed his decision to become a teacher is still directing Fred's belief in empowerment and the upliftment of communities; perhaps this sense of loyalty to one's community is the very reason why Brimstone is a fully fledged community asset.

It is not hard to understand why Fred can walk around proudly in his community – particularly on the days when dividends are paid out.

ADVICE TO ENTREPRENEURS

- You need to have the self-confidence to 'believe that you can do it'.
- You must have a vision, a dream.
- You must have faith in your product or service and 'believe that it will benefit the people to whom you sell it'.
- You have to have respect for your community and your clients.
- Don't expect to make money immediately – you should accept that it is a long, hard road, and that success is never achieved overnight.

CHAPTER 38

Koos Bekker

FOUNDER OF M-NET AND CHIEF EXECUTIVE OF NASPERS

Interview broadcast on 14 October 2012

Koos grew up on a maize farm near Heidelberg (Gauteng). He studied Law at Stellenbosch University and completed his LLB degree at the University of the Witwatersrand. After obtaining an MBA degree from Columbia University in the United States in 1984, he joined M-Net on his return to South Africa. In 1997 Koos was appointed chief executive of Naspers, a position he still holds today.

My interview with Hendrik du Toit, chief executive of Investec Asset Management, took place a few days before I was due to interview Koos. When I mentioned to Hendrik that I would be talking to Koos later that week, he remarked that Koos was, in his view, South Africa's greatest entrepreneur and our only real media and technology entrepreneur who can hold his own among the best in the world. According to Hendrik, Koos would be acclaimed much more prominently if he were not so strong and successful in the media industry; the other media groups in the country are all envious of his success, and his own group doesn't want to create the impression that they are trumpeting his achievements too loudly.

Before the interview, I was asked whether I knew what KSS stood for. Well, right at the start Koos made it clear that he wanted us to move from the venue that had been prepared for the shoot to a more informal venue – which was indeed done, because Koos Says So!

I started by asking him about his LLB degree and why he decided so soon after graduating not to pursue a legal career. It was when he started working as a public prosecutor in Soweto and had to deal with domestic violence cases, Koos explains, that he discovered he didn't like the court milieu. 'I like people who are happy and who build things, and business attracted me – I don't know why.' No one in his family had ever worked in the business world or studied in a business-related field. 'It was only really after starting to grapple with it that I realised I like the rhythm and the problems associated with business.'

Koos was newly married when he decided to do an MBA course at Columbia University in the United States. What prompted him to take this big step, he says, is that the MBA concept had basically originated in the United States and the best business schools were there. Studying at a top American university proved more demanding than what he had been exposed to in South Africa. Koos recalls that, during his first semester in a statistics class, it suddenly hit him that he was the worst-performing student in the class. 'I was right at the bottom, and the reason was, of course, that there were 50 extremely bright people in the class; you had to give your all just to pass the course because all 50 were trying to pass. So America helped me to sharpen up.'

When he looks back today, and also taking into account the world we now live in, would Koos still encourage young South Africans to go to the United States to study for an MBA? Definitely, he says with conviction. 'To understand your own country you have be outside it for a while, and to me the big benefit was to look back on South Africa from a different perspective and to say what is unique in our country, or what is lacking in our country.' In Koos's case, this was what led to the birth of M-Net and pay television – 'you saw something that existed in America but not in South Africa, and the question was, can we take the idea from there and apply it here?' In his view, therefore, it is 'very useful' to get that outsider's perspective on your country at a fairly early stage in your life, and then return with those insights.

After returning to South Africa with an MBA to his name, Koos decided in 1985 to look into the possibility of introducing pay television to the country. In America, he had started realising that 'pay television is a new phenomenon that's going to change the world'. A city like New York initially had four analogue television channels, and 'then the airwaves were full. You couldn't broadcast more channels.' The advent of cable television meant, however, that 'you could add another 50 or 100 channels and the way in which we watched television began fragmenting into CNN or Disney, namely, thematic channels'. The question that intrigued Koos was whether the same could be done outside America in a country without cable television. When they started M-Net, he says, 'it was the first pay-television service outside America'. The big challenge was: 'How do you take something that runs on cable in America and do it over the air in South Africa?'

At that stage 'we needed money, of course'. The press groups wanted to get involved in television, but the government of the day was intent on protecting the SABC from competition. According to Koos, the advantage of pay television was 'that you could go to the government and say, "Look, here are the six press groups in the country. Television is putting pressure on us. We'd like to invest in that field." If we also have television services, we would be tackling the SABC head-on and competing with them for advertising and so on. If we have pay television, on the other hand, it would be a more indirect form of competition. We would carry advertisements, but they wouldn't be our main source of income; our main source would be subscription, and that's a little less painful as far as competition is concerned.' And this argument worked, Koos adds.

But President PW Botha's government didn't want to make it worthwhile for M-Net to gather and broadcast news. 'We actually could if we wanted to,' Koos explains, 'but it was formulated in a very interesting way. He said we could broadcast news before five in the afternoon or after nine o'clock in the evening. That's tantamount to giving someone a restaurant licence and saying they're only allowed to serve meals when people aren't hungry.' This restriction was of course aimed at protecting the SABC news against competition, 'because the SABC felt the influence of the state fairly strongly, as it still does today'.

M-Net didn't have an easy start, however. Not many people realise how close they came to bankruptcy. After a few years, M-Net was in a desperate situation, losing about R3.5 million every month while their debts already amounted to about R37 million. The problem was that the shareholders had started to doubt the business model; if there was no improvement, the funding would have to be terminated. M-Net's eventual turnaround took place because of a technological breakthrough that all of a sudden rendered the business model viable.

According to Koos, they had made a calculation error by focusing on hotels and apartment blocks. Initially, there were a limited number of decoders (which were still manufactured by hand at the time), and the reasoning was that one decoder could serve an entire building. In the case of hotels, it worked 'and we earned something', but 'apartment blocks were a total fiasco'. What sunk them was a rule that 90% of the residents of a sectional-title complex had to agree to a new cost. Thus if an apartment block wanted pay television, the matter had to be put to the vote at a meeting of the body corporate. 'We never managed to get a 90% vote, and then it meant that no one was allowed to have it, the answer was no, and you got nothing.' Koos says they were 'on the verge of bankruptcy' when there was a change in their fortunes. The first factory-made decoders became available; they were able to put decoders into individual houses and apartments, and 'that brought about a complete change in the demand'. This was the breakthrough for M-Net. The business started growing, and 'about two years later we broke even'.

Today M-Net's DStv is one of the most successful pay-television businesses in the world, with over five million subscribers in 48 countries. I wanted to find out from the original entrepreneur who turned M-Net around what, in his view, has made DStv so successful. Koos reckons the key to their success is that they are very aware of what people want. 'In other words, you don't sit there and decide ideologically what you want to watch. People are very funny; you can offer them something you think they would like and it can be a total flop.' From the outset, DStv's approach has been that they analyse what people enjoy or find useful, give it to them, and discard the rest. When they started M-Net, they used to send people to Hollywood to watch movies and evaluate them. 'Then we realised this was just a total waste of time. Let's rather do it like this: South Africa's taste is more or less like America's. Let's construct a mathematical model based on how people actually respond. If a movie opens in America and it earns a certain amount of money in the first year, we classify it "A" and we pay, say, 30 American cents per subscriber. If it earns less, we pay 5 cents, and so on.' As a result, they buy movies without anyone watching them first and taking a subjective decision.

In 1997 Koos was in charge of the pay-television business, which he managed from the Netherlands, where his family lived. Ton Vosloo (now chairman of Naspers, then chairman of M-Net's board and chief executive of Naspers) approached Koos and offered him the job of chief executive of Naspers, as Ton wanted to retire. Naspers was one of the six press groups that had invested in M-Net; Ton acted as chairman of the press groups and, according to Koos, 'played a very positive role in our development'. When Ton asked Koos whether he wanted to succeed him as head of Naspers, Koos's response was that he was an entrepreneur; he wasn't interested in a salaried job. 'We then came to a rather unique agreement. I said, "Okay, I'll take the job. I don't want a salary or a bonus or a car or a medical scheme and such things; I'll do without a fixed package and you can fire me with 24 hours' notice, but I want 3% of the long-term value that is created above inflation." So we start on a certain day and there is a value. We measure it over five years and we say if you've only achieved this or only achieved this plus inflation, then you earn nothing; but you can get 3% of anything you achieve above that. That's more or less the structure.'

Today, Koos still works under 24 hours' notice, with no salary, benefits, medical scheme or pension, and can be dismissed summarily for no reason – and this after more than 15 years as chief executive. But the deal has worked well for everyone, particularly for the shareholders and also for Koos. When Koos became CEO of Naspers in 1997, the market value of the group was just over R5 billion. Today, Naspers has a market value of more than R220 billion – the value that has been added for shareholders easily exceeds R210 billion. Suddenly the 3% of the R210 billion looks like an excellent deal. When I ask Koos whether he had ever thought that the group would become so successful, he replies: 'You can't predict these things, can you? In the sense that the best you can do is to work every day – doing what comes to hand, and you don't know exactly where it will lead to. I must say, I have really enjoyed it. I enjoy media enormously, and the way in which the package is structured ... there's a wonderful saying: having a pistol held to your head concentrates the mind admirably. When you know that all you're going to get is the net value you create above inflation, you tell yourself every morning: how can we increase it? What can we do?'

When I inquire about highlights that stand out for him when he looks back on this growth trajectory, or milestones that contributed to his success, Koos's response is not quite what I expected. 'The highlight is very often the mess you make,' he says, 'because many times the lesson comes from the mistake.' He uses their first investment of R88 million in China as an example. 'Eighteen months later we had lost all our money, we had to fire 150 people, and we closed the business. We'd made a total hash of it. A complete failure. And then the team sat down and said, you can't make a bigger botch-up than this; what did we do wrong? We started analysing it and we said, one, we brought in Western managers and the Chinese are better managers – out. We went through all the points, drew our lessons from them, and what resulted from that were the subsequent Chinese investments that succeeded, such as Tencent, and so on.' He sums it up by saying: 'Very often that which you consider your success is actually an apple with a worm inside. Just give it three years, and that apple is rotten. And many times when you make a mistake, it already has concealed in it the solution to your next problem.'

I steered the conversation to 2007. Koos had been chief executive of Naspers for ten years, and he decided to take a year off. In the course of that year he visited 22 countries and gave lectures in some; his activities included a trip to Mongolia, a visit to the Amish community in Pennsylvania in the United States, and attending a course for CEOs at Harvard University. What lay behind this decision to take a year's sabbatical and travel the world? As Koos explains: 'Perhaps I became head of a business too early.' At that stage he had been head of a listed company for 20 years, with all the responsibilities and pressure that go with such a role. 'So I said that, before I die, I just want to bum around for a year and do things that interest me.' What interests him about the Amish is that they are opposed to technology. Koos's group 'introduces globalisation and technology into the world' and changes the life of, say, someone watching television at a remote mine in Katanga. The Amish, on the other hand, 'look to the past and say, "Technology is bad," so I felt I had to take a look at how they live and what one can learn from them.' What attracted him about Mongolia is that it is 'probably the most isolated country in the world, inhabited by Genghis Khan's descendants. So I was interested in seeing how they live today.'

The enthusiasm with which Koos talks about this topic prompts me to ask whether he would recommend such a breakaway period to others. As in the case of the American MBA, his answer is a succinct 'Definitely', and once again it relates to the value of a change of perspective. In his view, the risk of a long career in the business world is that you start taking yourself too seriously. 'People tend to accept your authority and eventually you start thinking that you're something special and that you have exceptional insight, and, in my experience, most business people are extremely ordinary.' Koos reckons that it does one a world of good 'to step out of your role for a while and walk to the supermarket without a title and in fact without a job'. The biggest mistakes, he believes, can often be ascribed to the fact that people 'become enmeshed in a set of facts and they're unable to look at things from outside that framework. Then you make strategic mistakes and take the whole company in a wrong direction. One advantage of stepping back a bit somewhere in your career is that you not only get perspective on the world and on your business, but sometimes you return and say, You know, we've been plodding along in this direction for five years. I think we should turn the whole story around and go in that direction. So, I believe a breakaway is a good thing.'

I wanted us to return to Naspers specifically. In one of their annual reports, he refers to the young engineers in the group as his combat generals. What does he mean by that? 'All the truly great internet breakthroughs were engineering breakthroughs,' Koos explains, 'and if you look at Steve Jobs or Mark Zuckerberg of Facebook or even the Zynga lot that are now developing games, they're all engineers. The social scientists and the BAs come in afterwards and they add a bit and expand a bit, but the real, the hard breakthroughs come from an engineering environment.' But the problem in South Africa, he adds, is that we don't produce nearly enough engineers and we don't honour engineers sufficiently.

Koos believes that there are only two types of people that create jobs: engineers and entrepreneurs. When it comes to the attributes of a good entrepreneur, he doesn't mince matters: 'The typical entrepreneur is a difficult person. He's not the sociable rugby captain with heaps of friends. He's a loner.' The challenge for Naspers is that they have to go in search of 'that little diamond', and 'then you often make a mistake and have to keep him on track, but it's not easy to keep him on track because he's so opinionated'. Koos reckons that he himself is like that, 'but it applies to any good entrepreneur. You're full of your own opinions and you don't want to listen to others; you're obstinate. So we have to try and find a balance where we accommodate this guy within our structure in such a way that he at least doesn't create absolute chaos, but at the same time give him enough space to realise himself and feel that it's actually his business.'

The world of technology and media is a fast-moving one. How do decision-making and planning work in such a constantly changing environment? He doesn't have a clue, declares Koos, 'and the interesting thing is, we've come to terms with the fact that you can't know'. Before the transition to 'this uncertain world', media companies usually had five-year plans. 'But what do you do in a new environment where you have no idea of what the world will look like in five years' time?'

What they try to construct is a model that Koos describes as follows: 'You tell someone, "Okay, you can't give me a five-year business plan because you don't know what the world will look like and I don't know either, because five years ago things like Twitter and Pinterest didn't exist. Predicting is useless. Let's see if you can provide a useful service." So all you need to do as an entrepreneur to convince us to give you money is to show us that you're useful, even if you make no money. Go and do something on the internet that really helps someone and then you return after a year and say, I help 20 million people every day. They don't pay me anything, but they come to me and I help them in the following way. Then we say, "Okay, we'll give you another $10 million, appoint another ten engineers and see whether you can be even more useful." Next year he returns and says he's now serving 50 million people – very, very, useful. Then we say, "Okay, change the business principle and see whether people are prepared to pay." Once people begin to pay, it's the start of a good business. In other words, you try to structure your system in such a way that it can work in a world where it's impossible to predict the future.'

Koos admits that he has changed. 'Ten years ago I would have told you my job is to guess what the world is going to look like in ten years' time. I've now made peace with the fact that I can't know, and we're trying to design a system that can give you direction within that uncertainty.'

Koos's excitement about the media and technology is palpable. What interests him so much about this field? He believes that, at least for his temperament, media is 'the nicest job in the world'. He says that he has 'calmed down over the years in the sense that when something wonderful happens, I don't get too excited and I tell myself we've been there too many times. It doesn't look as good as it really is. And when things are tough and everything turns against you, then you say, Well, I've been there before too. I've seen how the thing can turn around.'

When he looks back on his career, two things stand out for him as far as enjoying his work is concerned. The first has been working with 'nice people'. 'We've had exceptional people: engineers, financial people, marketing people, nice directors. It's a pleasure working in a milieu of people that you like.' The second aspect that he singles out is the complexity of their work. 'I get immense enjoyment from working in a complex world with a multitude of things all moving at the same time. Then I think that, if I were a bit smarter, I would be able to do a better job; this job is actually too complex for me. When I go home in the evenings I feel that I've really been stretched to the maximum and that if I had slightly better brains I would be able to do better, but this was the best I could do.'

I agree wholeheartedly with Hendrik du Toit; Koos is a remarkable entrepreneur, and his career seems to offer clear and convincing proof that only entrepreneurs and engineers are ultimately responsible for real progress.

WHAT ADVICE WOULD KOOS BEKKER GIVE TO A 20-YEAR-OLD KOOS BEKKER TODAY?

- As a point of departure, he says, 'the first bit of advice is, Don't listen to anyone. The entrepreneurs I know are all exceptionally stubborn people, and it's almost essential that you believe in something that you think you can do better than anyone else in the world.'
- Find out what you really like. As the writer Somerset Maugham puts it: 'Finding something that you really love doing and then getting someone to pay you to do it.'

- Other people give you 'the conventional advice and often, especially in business, the best way to make money is actually by going against the grain. To do something that others don't want to do. If no one wants to drive the night cart, then you go and drive the night cart – that going-against-the-grain attitude works quite well in business.'
- It is worth one's while to analyse big social movements and trends and to say: where is the world going? 'It's easier to achieve success in an area where the tide is rising underneath you.'

Seven golden rules for success

What stands out clearly from the 38 stories in this book is
that there is no such thing as a single miracle recipe that will
guarantee business success. Nor are there short cuts or quick
fixes. Yet there is a golden thread of common attributes and
approaches that consistently comes to the fore. From this
'golden thread' I have drawn seven points that, in my view, can be
summed up as the golden rules for success.

1. Passion

All these star performers are passionate about what they do. They love
going to work and derive pleasure from their jobs. It is unlikely that you
will be successful, let alone be happy in your career, in a position or
an industry that doesn't excite you. Rather spend more time on finding
and developing your own passion than merely following what others
are doing.

2. Knowledge, hours and hard work

Many of the business leaders and entrepreneurs referred directly or
indirectly to the '10 000-hour rule' Malcolm Gladwell talks about in his
book *Outliers: The Story of Success*. According to Gladwell, the key to
success in any field is, to a large extent, a matter of practising a specific
task or skill for about 10 000 hours before you become expert at it. You
simply have to 'put in the hours' and set yourself apart from others by
gaining more knowledge and experience than them and by working
harder than them. There is no substitute for technical knowledge
combined with hard work and thorough preparation.

3. A vision

You need to have a longer-term vision for yourself and for your business, a dream that inspires you and gives you the strength to persevere. This vision then becomes the guideline in terms of which you steer your business; all decisions and transactions should be in line with the vision and contribute to its realisation. When you look more closely at successes that are frequently attributed to luck, you find that the opportunity presented itself within the context of a vision of the future. With that focus, the person was able to spot the value in the opportunity and to exploit it.

4. Delegate to the right team

None of these business leaders and entrepreneurs could have accomplished their goals without teamwork. While it is crucial to choose the right people for your team, you also need to empower them within a creative and constructive organisational culture. Appoint expert subject specialists who complement your own weaknesses, and allow them to contribute positively to the business.

5. Principles, your own opinion and self-confidence

Every businessperson must have a set of values or a moral code that guides the way he or she behaves and does business. In addition to integrity and firmness of principle, you should have the self-confidence to express your opinions and take a stand, to think for yourself and to believe that you can succeed. The fact that others disagree with you doesn't mean that you are wrong; in many cases, particularly when it comes to innovation, it may actually mean that you are right! These principles will ultimately determine how your clients, your business partners and your employees see you and whether they will support you on your road to success.

6. Financial and compliance management

You must know at all times exactly what the financial position is within your business, specifically, what the cash flow looks like and what the risks are that could impact negatively upon the business. Regardless of whether it is a big company, a growing business or a small enterprise in its infancy, make sure that controls and reporting are fully up to date and documented. It stands to reason that you need to introduce and keep up the necessary procedures and controls, otherwise you won't be aware of danger signals.

7. A positive attitude towards change and opportunities

The point of departure should be to see every change as a possible opportunity. You have to keep abreast of trends in your business environment, in society at large and in the global arena, specifically with a view to identifying opportunities in this uncertain and changing environment.

The general impression I gained is that this group of business leaders and entrepreneurs are more optimistic than the average South African, not only about their businesses but also about the future. It is striking how many of the success stories and real growth of these businesses took place after 1994; some of my guests stated frankly that part of their success could be directly attributed to the political and economic changes. Perhaps, as a group, they are more positive because they are used to taking a longer-term perspective and are more aware of the fact that South Africa's challenges and problems are not unique. It may also be because they are inclined to take personal control of their circumstances and have learnt from experience that setbacks and obstacles don't have to impede you, provided that you are prepared to search for solutions and to carry them through.

ACKNOWLEDGMENTS

Having a plan is one thing, but the challenge is to make the plan work!

Sakegesprek began as an idea. For transforming the idea into a TV programme, I have to thank my colleague Warren Ingram and my friends André du Plessis (he's the person whose hand I shake in front of the JSE building at the start of the programme) and Pieter Hurter, as well as my school friend Louis Eksteen. I also owe thanks to my brother Maas who not only gave me valuable input but also introduced me to Gwen Bezuidenhout, who very enthusiastically arranged a meeting with Karen Meiring. From the outset, Karen Meiring (head of the kykNET channel) and Marida Swanepoel (supervisory producer, who also created the name *Sakegesprek met Theo Vorster*) have supported the programme wholeheartedly.

As far as the writing of the book is concerned, I have to single out the part played by Linde Dietrich as editor. I will never try to pass myself off as a writer; the person who ultimately made the book readable was Linde. In the course of this process I also gained a thorough understanding of the role of a publisher, and in this regard I am delighted that Ingeborg Pelser and Jonathan Ball Publishers chose me.

My deepest gratitude is due to my family for their input and their unflagging support – specifically my parents (who contact me after every broadcast and give me their honest opinion), my wife and my daughter, who record every programme in order to discuss it with me. Compiling a television programme and writing a book are both activities that take up much family time – whether evenings, weekends or a December holiday spent in front of a computer. Without the support, encouragement and belief of Anneke (my wife) and Mia (my daughter), neither the TV series nor the book would have been possible!

To everyone who has taken the trouble to send me comments – thank you very much. I read all the feedback and take it to heart!